M000166461

THE ROYAL COURT THEATRE PRESENTS

Bad Roads

by Natal'ya Vorozhbit
Translated by Sasha Dugdale

Bad Roads was first performed at the Royal Court Jerwood Theatre Upstairs, Sloane Square, on Wednesday 15 November 2017.

Bad Roads is presented as part of International Playwrights: A Genesis Foundation Project.

Bad Roads

by Natal'ya Vorozhbit

Translated by Sasha Dugdale

CAST (in alphabetical order)

Girl 3/Woman 2 **Ronke Adekoluejo**
Woman/Girl 2 **Kate Dickie**
Headteacher/Vasya **Vincent Ebrahim**
Woman 1/Vasya's Wife **Anne Lacey**
Soldier 1/He **Tadhg Murphy**
Commander/Soldier 2 **Mike Noble**
Girl 1/She **Ria Zmitrowicz**

Director **Vicky Featherstone**
Designer **Camilla Clarke**
Lighting Designer **Natasha Chivers**
Music & Sound Designer **Nick Powell**
Production Manager **Marty Moore**
Costume Supervisor **Gina Lee**
Associate Director **Grace Gummer**
Assistant Director **Segen Yosef**
Casting Director **Amy Ball**
International Director **Elyse Dodgson**
Associate Director (International) **Sam Pritchard**
International Assistant **Sarah Murray**
Stage Managers **Lizzie Donaghy, Osnat Koblenz**

The Royal Court would like to thank the following for their help with this production:

The British Council, The Young Vic Theatre and Paul Wanklin.

Bad Roads

by Natal'ya Vorozhbit

Translated by Sasha Dugdale

Natal'ya Vorozhbit (Writer)

For the Royal Court: **The Khomenko Family Chronicles, Maidan: Voices from the Uprising.**

Other theatre includes: **Vy (Maksim Golenko, Magdeburg); Shame (Artishok/Almaty, Kazakhstan); Take the Rubbish Out, Sasha (National Theatre of Scotland/Òran Mór); The Grain Store (RSC); Demons, Galka Motalko (Moscow/National Theatre of Latvia).**

Films include: **Cyborgs, Voroshilovgrad, Galka Motalko.**

Awards include: **Eureka Prize (Galka Motalko); Golden Mask for Docudrama (Vy).**

Natal'ya was born in Kiev and studied at the Moscow Literary Institute. She took part in Royal Court workshops in Moscow and attended the Royal Court International Residency in 2005. She is the co-founder of the Theatre of the Displaced in Kiev and curator of the Class Act project in Ukraine.

Ronke Adekoluejo (Girl 3/Woman 2)

Theatre includes: **The Mountaintop (Young Vic); Twelfth Night (Filter); The Oresteia (Home, Manchester); Pride & Prejudice (Crucible, Sheffield); The House That Will Not Stand, The Colby Sisters of Pittsburgh Pennsylvania (Tricycle); Anon (WNO); Random (Crooked Path).**

Television includes: **Doctor Who, NW, Cold Feet, Sick Note, Josh, Chewing Gum, Suspects, The Forgiving Earth.**

Film includes: **Been So Long, Ready Player One, One Crazy Thing, Lascivious Grace, Broken.**

Natasha Chivers (Lighting Designer)

For the Royal Court: **Fireworks, Adler & Gibb, The Mistress Contract, Gastronauts, The Djinns of Eidgah, That Face (& West End).**

Theatre includes: **1984 (West End/Broadway); Hamlet, Oresteia (Almeida/West End); The House They Grew Up In (Chichester Festival); Sunset at the Villa Thalia, Statement of Regret (National); The Taming of the Shrew (Globe); Happy Days (Crucible, Sheffield); Green Snake (National Theatre of China); The Radicalisation of Bradley Manning (National Theatre Wales); Macbeth (& Broadway), 27, The Wolves in the Walls, Home (National Theatre of Scotland); Sunday in the Park with George (West End).**

Dance includes: **Strapless (Royal Ballet).**

Awards include: **Theatre Award UK for Best Design (Happy Days); Olivier Award for Best Lighting Design (Sunday in the Park with George).**

Camilla Clarke (Designer)

As designer, for the Royal Court: **Human Animals.**

As associate designer, for the Royal Court: **B, Victory Condition.**

As designer, other theatre includes: **Frogman (Curious Directive/Traverse); No Place for a Woman (503); Wind Resistance (Lyceum, Edinburgh); Seagulls (Volcano).**

Opera includes: **The Day After, Trial by Jury (ENO).**

Awards include: **Linbury Prize for Stage Design; Lord Williams Prize for Design; The Prince of Wales Design Scholarship.**

Kate Dickie (Woman/Girl 2)

Theatre includes: **Our Town (Almeida); Aalst (Soho/UK & international tours); Any Given Day (Traverse).**

Television includes: **Game of Thrones, The Pillars of the Earth, Five Daughters, Vera, One of Us, The Frankenstein Chronicles, Midwinter of the Spirit, By Any Means, The Escape Artist, Injustice, Dive, New Tricks, Garrows Law, He Kills Coppers, Taggart, The Vice, Tinsel Town.**

Film includes: **The Witch, Couple in a Hole, The Silent Storm, For Those in Peril, Filth, Prometheus, Shell, Now is Good, Outcast, Donkeys, Somers Town, Red Road, Summer, Operator.**

Awards include: **BAFTA (Scotland) Award for Best Actress (Couple in a Hole); Spirit of Scotland Screen Award; British Independent Film Award for Best Actress, Festival Nouveau Cinema Montréal Award for Best Actress, BAFTA (Scotland) Award for Best Actress (Red Road).**

Sasha Dugdale (Translator)

For the Royal Court: **Plasticine, Black Milk, Ladybird, Terrorism, Playing the Victim, Maidan: Voices from the Uprising, The Khomenko Family Chronicles.**

Other theatre includes: **The Grain Store (RSC).**

Radio includes: **The Cherry Orchard, Three Sisters.**

Awards include: **Cholmondeley Prize for Contribution to Poetry; Forward Prize for Best Single Poem (Joy).**

Sasha is a poet and translator. She has published four collections of her own poems as well as two collections of translations of Russian poetry. Sasha worked for the British Council in Russia where she set up the Russian New Writing Project with the Royal Court.

Vincent Ebrahim (Headteacher/Vasya)

For the Royal Court: **The Djinns of Eidgah, Credible Witness.**

Other theatre includes: **Occupational Hazards, Nathan the Wise (Hampstead); Ramayana (& Birmingham Rep), Dara, Behind the Beautiful Forevers, Tartuffe, Little Clay Cart, Fanshen (National); The Empress, Real Dreams, The Danton Affair (RSC); The Great Game (Tricycle/International tour); A Midsummer Night's Dream (Tara Arts/Lyric).**

Television includes: **40 North, Casualty, Hoff the Record, Hollyoaks, Doctors, The Old Guys, Compulsion, The Kumars at Number 42, New Street Law, After You've Gone, Meet the Magoons, The Lenny Henry Show, Holby City, Bedtime, Doctors, Clocking Off.**

Film includes: **Allied, The Physician, Material, The Curse of the Wererabbit.**

Radio includes: **The Last Missionary of Kanaipur, Mrs Sidhu Investigates: Murder with Masala, The End of Sand, Occupational Hazards, The Odyssey Project, Something Understood, Tumanbay, Revelation, Oedipus the King, School Drama, Dark Fire, Everyday Story of Afghan Folk.**

Vicky Featherstone (Director)

For the Royal Court: **Victory Condition, X, Cyprus Avenue (& Abbey, Dublin), How To Hold Your Breath, God Bless the Child, Maidan: Voices from the Uprising, The Mistress Contract, The Ritual Slaughter of Gorge Mastromas; Untitled Matriarch Play, The President Has Come to See You (Open Court Weekly Rep).**

Other theatre includes: **What If Women Ruled the World? (Manchester International Festival); Our Ladies of Perpetual Succour (& National/West End/International tour), Enquirer (co-director), An Appointment with the Wicker Man, 27, The Wheel, Somersaults, Wall of Death: A Way of Life (co-director), The Miracle Man, Empty, Long Gone Lonesome (National Theatre of Scotland); Cockroach (National Theatre of Scotland/Traverse); 365 (National Theatre of Scotland/Edinburgh International Festival); Mary Stuart (National Theatre of Scotland/Citizens/Royal Lyceum, Edinburgh); The Wolves in the Walls (co-director) (Improbable/National Theatre of Scotland/Tramway/Lyric,**

Hammersmith/UK tour/New Victory, New York); **The Small Things, Pyrenees, On Blindness, The Drowned World, Tiny Dynamite, Crazy Gary's Mobile Disco, Splendour, Riddance, The Cosmonaut's Last Message to the Woman He Once Loved in the Former Soviet Union, Crave (Paines Plough).**

Television includes: **Where the Heart Is, Silent Witness.**

Vicky was Artistic Director of Paines Plough 1997-2005 and the inaugural Artistic Director of the National Theatre of Scotland 2005-2012. Vicky is the Artistic Director of the Royal Court.

Grace Gummer (Associate Director)

As director, for the Royal Court: **Sense, Theatre from the Windows, Theatre Uncontained, Stories from My Mother (Open Court); H, Typical, The Higher We Go, The System (Big Idea).**

As assistant director, for the Royal Court: **Victory Condition, Road, Anatomy of a Suicide, Nuclear War, The Kid Stays in the Picture (& Complicite), The Sewing Group, We Anchor in Hope, Primetime 2016.**

As director, other theatre includes: **Butter (Vault Festival); Liberator (503 RWR); Anonymous Anonymous (The Space); Dead Dove, Pineapple Juice (Brockley Jack).**

As associate director, other theatre includes: **Re:Home, Drawing Play (Yard).**

As assistant director, other theatre includes: **Beyond Caring (& National), Lines, Qudz (Yard); Walking the Tightrope (Theatre Delicatessen).**

Grace is Trainee Director at the Royal Court.

Anne Lacey (Woman 1/Vasya's Wife)

Theatre includes: **The Lying Kind (Tron); Cuttin' a Rug, Therese Raquin, The Killing of Sister George (Citizens); Diana of Dobsons (New Vic); Disturbed, Happy Hour (Òran Mór); Uncle Vanya (West Yorkshire Playhouse); Bondagers, Dark Earth, Straw Chair, Distracted, The Artist Man & the Mother Woman (Traverse); Earthquakes in London (National); Victoria (RSC); David Copperfield (Dundee Rep); Blithe Spirit (Perth Rep); Swan Song (Print Room); Mary Queen of Scots Got Her Head Chopped Off (Communicado).**

Television includes: **Hamish Macbeth, Holby City, Monarch of the Glen, Stacey Stone, Rab C Nesbitt, Tinsel Town, Deacon Brodie, Knowing the Score, Doctor Finlay, Sweet Nothings.**

Film includes: **Wiyuld, The Bedford's, My Life So Far, This Year's Love, Strictly Sinatra, Harry Potter & the Goblet of Fire, And Then I Was French.**

Radio includes: **Reacher's Point, The Poet & the Echo, Tender is the Night, Hunger, Gold, Blown Away, The Cherry Blossom Whisky Company, Sullom Voe, Quartet, Mr Anwar's Farewell to Stornaway.**

Tadhg Murphy (Soldier 1/He)

Theatre includes: **Ballyturk, Three Sisters (& USA tour), Aristocrats (Abbey, Dublin); Our Country's Good (National); Romeo & Juliet, Mrs. Warren's Profession, Hay Fever (& Spoleto Festival, Charleston USA), Da, The Speckled People, The Real Thing (Gate, Dublin); How These Desperate Men Talk, MedEia (Corcadorca); Waiting For Godot (Gaiety, Dublin/USA tour); The Cripple of Inishmaan, The Walworth Farce (UK & international tours), Penelope (Druid); The Taming of the Shrew (Rough Magic).**

Television includes: **Guerrilla, Will, Black Sails, Vikings, Seachtar na Cásca, An Crisis, The Clinic, Love is the Drug, No Tears.**

Film includes: **The Secret Market, Lost in the Living, Pride & Joy, Jelly Baby, Boy Eats Girl, Alexander.**

Radio includes: **The Plough & the Stars, The Finnegans, The Colleen & the Cowboy.**

Mike Noble (Commander/Soldier 2)

For the Royal Court: **Road.**

Other theatre includes: **Game (Almeida); The Curious Incident of the Dog in the Night-Time, Port (National); Mudlarks (HighTide/Bush); Punk Rock (Lyric, Hammersmith/Royal Exchange, Manchester).**

Television includes: **Home Fires, Mr Selfridge, Grantchester, Prisoner's Wives.**

Film includes: **Dark River, The Siege of Jadotville, Rules of the Game, Kill Command, Jack Ryan, Jadoo, Private Peaceful, World War Z, Gambit.**

Nick Powell (Music & Sound Designer)

For the Royal Court: **The Ferryman (& West End), X, Unreachable, The Mistress Contract, The Nether (& West End), The Ritual Slaughter of Gorge Mastromas, Talk Show, Narrative, Get Santa! (co-creator), The Vertical Hour, The Priory, Relocated.**

Other theatre includes: **People, Places & Things (Stadsteatern, Stockholm); City of Glass (59 Productions/Lyric, Hammersmith); Alice in Wonderland (Lyceum, Edinburgh); Running Wild, Peter Pan, All My Sons, Lord of the Flies, The Crucible (Regent's Park Open Air/UK tour); The Tempest (Norfolk & Norwich Festival); The Haunting of Hill House (Liverpool Playhouse); Lanark: A Life in Three Acts (Citizens/

Edinburgh International Festival); Wolf Hall/ Bring Up The Bodies (RSC/West End/Broadway); Dunsinane (RSC/Tour); 27, The Wheel, The Wonderful World of Dissocia (National Theatre of Scotland/Edinburgh International Festival); Of Mice & Men (Birmingham Rep/Tour); Show 6 – Secret Theatre (Lyric, Hammersmith/ Edinburgh Festival Fringe); Othello (National); A Life of Galileo, Richard III, The Drunks, God in Ruins (RSC); Urtain, Marat-Sade, Los Macbez (Animalario/CDN Madrid); Paradise (Rhur Triennale), Bank On It (Theatre Rites); 'Tis Pity She's A Whore (Cheek by Jowl); Penumbra, Tito Andronico (Animalario, Madrid); The Danton Affair (Stadsteater, Gothenburg); The Wolves in the Walls (Improbable/National Theatre of Scotland/Tramway/Lyric, Hammersmith/ UK tour/New Victory, New York); Realism (Edinburgh International Festival/National Theatre of Scotland); Panic (Improbable); The Family Reunion (Donmar).**

Awards include: **Animalario Award for Best Musical Composition for Scenic Arts Premios Max (Urtain).**

Nick also writes extensively for TV and film. He is half of OSKAR, who have released two albums and produced installations for the V&A and CCA, as well as written live soundtracks for Prada in Milan. He was worked with on installations for the 2017 opening ceremony of the Edinburgh International Festival and the Guggenheim Museum, Bilbao. He presented his chamber piece The Arctic Project at the Birmingham Rep with the City of Birmingham Symphony Orchestra.

Segen Yosef (Assistant Director)

As director, theatre includes: **Untitled (Platform); Black? British? Black British?, Black Aerosol, Torn Between the Two (New Diorama); Freshy (Shoreditch Town Hall).**

As assistant director, theatre includes: **Boat (BAC).**

As co-director, theatre includes: **The Common (Theatre Delicatessen).**

Ria Zmitrowicz (Girl 1/She)

For the Royal Court: **X.**

Other theatre includes: **Plastic (Theatre Royal, Bath); Four Minutes Twelve Seconds (Hampstead/Trafalgar Studios); The Crucible (Royal Exchange, Manchester); Arcadia (ETT/ Theatre Royal, Brighton); God's Property, NT Connections (Soho); Chapel Street (Bush/Old Red Lion); Cortae (Talawa); Skanky (Arcola).**

Television includes: **Three Girls, Mr Selfridge, Youngers, Nightshift, The Midnight Beast, Murder on the Home Front, Whitechapel.**

Film includes: **Kill Your Friends, Jellyfish.**

THE ROYAL COURT THEATRE

The Royal Court Theatre is the writers' theatre. It is a leading force in world theatre for energetically cultivating writers – undiscovered, emerging and established.

Through the writers, the Royal Court is at the forefront of creating restless, alert, provocative theatre about now. We open our doors to the unheard voices and free thinkers that, through their writing, change our way of seeing.

Over 120,000 people visit the Royal Court in Sloane Square, London, each year and many thousands more see our work elsewhere through transfers to the West End and New York, UK and international tours, digital platforms, our residencies across London, and our site-specific work. Through all our work we strive to inspire audiences and influence future writers with radical thinking and provocative discussion.

The Royal Court's extensive development activity encompasses a diverse range of writers and artists and includes an ongoing programme of writers' attachments, readings, workshops and playwriting groups. Twenty years of the International Department's pioneering work around the world means the Royal Court has relationships with writers on every continent.

Within the past sixty years, John Osborne, Samuel Beckett, Arnold Wesker, Ann Jellicoe, Howard Brenton and David Hare have started their careers at the Court. Many others including Caryl Churchill, Athol Fugard, Mark Ravenhill, Simon Stephens, debbie tucker green, Sarah Kane – and, more recently, Lucy Kirkwood, Nick Payne, Penelope Skinner and Alistair McDowall – have followed.

The Royal Court has produced many iconic plays from Laura Wade's **Posh** to Jez Butterworth's **Jerusalem** and Martin McDonagh's **Hangmen**.

Royal Court plays from every decade are now performed on stage and taught in classrooms and universities across the globe.

It is because of this commitment to the writer that we believe there is no more important theatre in the world than the Royal Court.

Supported using public funding by
ARTS COUNCIL ENGLAND

INTERNATIONAL PLAYWRIGHTS
AT THE ROYAL COURT THEATRE

Over the last two decades the Royal Court Theatre has led the way in the development and production of new international plays, facilitating work at grass-roots level and developing exchanges which brings UK writers and directors to work with emerging artists around the world. Through a programme of long-term workshops and residencies, in London and abroad, a creative dialogue now exists with theatre practitioners from over 70 countries, working in over 40 languages, most recently Argentina, Chile, China, Cuba, Georgia, India, Lebanon, Mexico, Palestine, Russia, South Africa, Syria, Turkey, Ukraine, Uruguay and Zimbabwe. All of these development projects are supported by the Genesis Foundation and the British Council.

The Royal Court Theatre has produced dozens of new international plays through this programme since 1997, most recently **B** by Guillermo Calderón (Chile) in 2017, **I See You** by Mongiwekhaya (South Africa) in 2016, **Fireworks** by Dalia Taha (Palestine) in 2015, **The Djinns of Eidgah** by Abhishek Majumdar (India) and **A Time to Reap** by Anna Wakulik (Poland) in 2013, **Remembrance Day** by Aleksey Scherbak (Latvia) and **Our Private Life** by Pedro Miguel Rozo (Colombia) in 2011, and **Disconnect** by Anupama Chandrasekhar (India) in 2010.

ROYAL COURT AND UKRAINE

Natal'ya Vorozhbit was the first Ukrainian writer to work with the Royal Court when she took part in workshops with Russian language writers in Moscow in 2004. She attended the Royal Court International Residency in 2005 and we produced her short play **The Khomenko Family Chronicles**, translated by Sasha Dugdale, in the International Season in the Jerwood Theatre Upstairs in 2007. In 2010 a second Ukrainian writer, Anna Yablonskaya, took part in the International Residency. Anna was tragically killed in the 2011 bombing of Domodedovo Airport. The Royal Court staged a reading of her play **Pagans**, translated by Rory Mullarkey, in the 2011 International Season.

In 2011 the Royal Court embarked on a long term project with writers from all parts of Ukraine in a joint workshop with writers from Georgia, supported by the British Council. These workshops were led by playwrights April De Angelis, Nick Payne and Rory Mullarkey and directors Ramin Gray and Caroline Steinbeis. In March 2013, three Ukrainian writers took part in staged readings of their new plays in the Jerwood Theatre Upstairs: Mariam Agamian,

Established by John Studzinski 16 years ago, the Genesis Foundation works in partnership with the leaders of prestigious UK arts organisations such as the Royal Court, The Sixteen, Welsh National Opera and the Young Vic. Its largest funding commitment is to programmes that support directors, playwrights and musicians in the early stages of their professional lives.

In addition it awards scholarships to exceptional student actors at LAMDA and commissions stimulating new works, from choral compositions to light installations.

In 2015 the Genesis Foundation launched its first partnership outside the UK, funding residencies for playwrights at New York's Signature Theatre.

ROYAL

COMING UP IN 2017/18

24 Nov–30 Dec
INTERNATIONAL PLAYWRIGHTS: A GENESIS
FOUNDATION PROJECT

Goats
By Liwaa Yazji
Translated by Katharine Halls

6 Dec–23 Dec

Grimly Handsome
By Julia Jarcho

8 Jan–20 Jan

My Mum's A Twat
By Anoushka Warden

9 Jan–27 Jan
ROYAL COURT THEATRE, OUT OF JOINT
AND OCTAGON THEATRE BOLTON

Rita, Sue and Bob Too
By Andrea Dunbar

31 Jan–10 Mar

Gundog
By Simon Longman

8 Feb–10 Mar

Girls & Boys
By Dennis Kelly

Tickets from £12
royalcourttheatre.com

Supported using public funding by
ARTS COUNCIL ENGLAND

Sloane Square London, SW1W 8AS ⊖ Sloane Square
⇌ Victoria Station 🐦 royalcourt 🅵 royalcourttheatre

GUNDOG is part of the Royal Court's Jerwood
New Playwrights programme, supported by

JERWOOD **CHARITABLE** FOUNDATION

Genesis FOUNDATION

COURT

ROYAL COURT SUPPORTERS

The Royal Court is a registered charity and not-for-profit company. We need to raise £1.5 million every year in addition to our core grant from the Arts Council and our ticket income to achieve what we do.

We have significant and longstanding relationships with many generous organisations and individuals who provide vital support. Royal Court supporters enable us to remain the writers' theatre, find stories from everywhere and create theatre for everyone.

We can't do it without you.

PUBLIC FUNDING

Arts Council England, London
British Council

TRUSTS & FOUNDATIONS

The Bryan Adams Charitable
  Trust
The Austin & Hope
  Pilkington Trust
Martin Bowley Charitable
  Trust
Gerald Chapman Fund
CHK Charities
The City Bridge Trust
The Clifford Chance
  Foundation
Cockayne - Grants for the
  Arts
The Ernest Cook Trust
The Nöel Coward Foundation
Cowley Charitable Trust
The Eranda Rothschild
  Foundation
Lady Antonia Fraser for
  The Pinter Commission
Genesis Foundation
The Golden Bottle Trust
The Haberdashers' Company
The Paul Hamlyn Foundation
Roderick & Elizabeth Jack
Jerwood Charitable
  Foundation
Kirsh Foundation
The Mackintosh Foundation
The Andrew Lloyd Webber
  Foundation
The London Community
  Foundation

John Lyon's Charity
Clare McIntyre's Bursary
The Andrew W. Mellon
  Foundation
The Mercers' Company
The Portrack Charitable Trust
The David & Elaine Potter
  Foundation
The Richard Radcliffe
  Charitable Trust
Rose Foundation
Royal Victoria Hall Foundation
The Sackler Trust
The Sobell Foundation
John Thaw Foundation
The Garfield Weston
  Foundation

CORPORATE SPONSORS

Aqua Financial Solutions Ltd
Bloomberg
Cadogan Estates
Colbert
Edwardian Hotels, London
Fever-Tree
Gedye & Sons
Kirkland & Ellis
  International LLP
Kudos
MAC
Room One
Sister Pictures
Sky Drama

BUSINESS MEMBERS

Annoushka
Auerbach & Steele
  Opticians
CNC – Communications &
  Network Consulting
Cream
Lansons
Left Bank Pictures
Rockspring Property
  Investment Managers
Tetragon Financial Group

For more information or to become a foundation or business supporter contact Camilla Start: camillastart@royalcourttheatre.com/020 7565 5064.

Supported using public funding by
ARTS COUNCIL ENGLAND

"There are no spaces, no rooms in my opinion, with a greater legacy of fearlessness, truth and clarity than this space."

Simon Stephens, Associate Playwright

The Royal Court invests in the future of the theatre, offering writers the support, time and resources to find their voices and tell their stories, asking the big questions and responding to the issues of the moment.

As a registered charity, the Royal Court relies on the generous support of individuals to seek out, develop and nurture new voices. Please join us in Writing The Future by donating today.

You can donate online at royalcourttheatre.com/donate or via our donation box in the Bar & Kitchen.

We can't do it without you.

To find out more about the different ways in which you can be involved please contact Charlotte Cole on 020 7565 5049 / charlottecole@royalcourttheatre.com

Writing the Future

BAD ROADS

Natal'ya Vorozhbit

Translated by Sasha Dugdale

Characters

WOMAN
TEENAGE GIRL ONE
TEENAGE GIRL TWO
TEENAGE GIRL THREE
WOMAN ONE
SOLDIER ONE
HEADTEACHER
COMMANDER
SOLDIER TWO
WOMAN TWO
HE
SHE
GIRL
VASYA'S WIFE
VASYA

This text went to press before the end of rehearsals and so may differ slightly from the play as performed.

1.

Quote marks denote speeches by other characters within the monologue.

WOMAN. When I first travelled to the Donbas region they asked me to fill out a form and on the form I had to describe myself, my appearance, any particular features. Just in case something happened to me, so they could identify the body. But I don't have any particular features. So I'll describe everything.

My name is Natasha. I'm forty years old already. I have a small build so I look younger. And I have a large nose, beautiful brown eyes, thin lips, small breasts and thin arms and legs. I have some ugly scars on my body, one on my belly from an operation, and another on my buttock, from an injection I had at school. I'm not in great shape, because of all the stress and not looking after myself properly. I'm pale, and sometimes I can feel my heart racing. You'll call me 'Sparrow'.

Now I'll describe you.

Your name is Sergei and you're thirty-eight. Average height. Although, no, you're shorter than average. You're strong, trim, upright. You look older than you are. You've got a strong voice, harsh grey bristle on your head. You've got brown eyes, and when I look into them I feel as if they have taken me hostage and left me in a dark basement, where some unknown terror is about to begin. I desperately want to look into your eyes. I desperately want you to like me.

I've already fallen for you.

I fell for you, but not at first sight. It was the second time. I was interviewing you in a café in Kiev. It was a warm winter. I'd dressed up, I was wearing my red coat, you were in uniform. I said 'you look good'. A muscle twitched on your face and I realised you were pleased. You're this hero. You're talking about the war, about Donetsk airport, which is what I was researching. You start drawing on a napkin the old and new airport terminals, the position of the enemy, list the names of weapons. I pretend I'm following, but I'm not really. You're remote, inaccessible, but my interest in the war excites you. This is my only road to you. You're drawing the only road back from the airport. Your hands are coarse.

'See, Natalya, the storm brigade had been relieved and they were leaving along this road here. And here were the rocket launchers and here the guns, and here are the armed personnel carriers and there's a lot of firepower concentrated here, and this is one of our tanks burning. We had a casualty and three fatalities that day. Four of the enemy died on the mine wires.'

You are talking and I am watching your lips.

And then I go to the cinema and watch a documentary about the war. You'd just told me about it, and then I go and watch a film about a war you were in. Explosions going off around you. You're carrying a gun, you're filthy. Right in front of us a soldier dies, a young guy. And then there's a casualty, and then another dead body. And you're shouting orders. I can't take it all in, that these explosions and shots and deaths aren't just faked for the film, that the dirt on your face isn't make-up. That you aren't just some ripped Brad Pitt lookalike. And that you really have killed another person.

I try to pray to the picture of Mary in one of the cathedrals at the Vydubychi Monastery. I don't really know how to pray, but all the same the tears are streaming down my face. I pray for my mother, my daughter, for peace in Ukraine, I light a candle for all the dead. But I am not crying for them, let's be honest, I'm crying for you. I want love with you. But I can't do it, I'm ashamed to ask her for that.

But Mary understood, and passed up my message. She probably said: this woman wants to suffer. Help her. And then you rang and said, 'come with me to the zone. I'll show you the front line. Would you like to?' Who'd turn down an offer like that? Everyone wants to be on the front line. I made the decision in an instant. I didn't take hot coffee and cold chicken and all the things a woman should take when she sets off with a man on a long journey. So we ate disgusting hot dogs in petrol stations and drank coffee with the sour taste of vomit. You don't listen to music in your car with its camouflage paint, you smoke and you don't say much. Ahead of us the road breaks up. Ahead is the east and the war. You and me, two complete strangers. Completely different species. How come I feel so calm, so happy?

You tell me about the battle for Donetsk airport, the battle I'm researching.

'The separatists wanted to take the airport in time for Putin's birthday as a present for him. They were going to use this rocket launcher, Buratino, it's like a weapon of mass destruction, it destroys every living thing within a radius of three k. Our commanding officers weren't confirming this openly, but they weren't denying it either. But we were pretty convinced by the way the separatists were evacuating weapons and people away from the airport. In just a few hours the airport, which had been under fire and siege for months, was no longer surrounded. It's like, there's this terrible silence all round. The first silence in that airport. All night we were preparing for the end. I rang my daughter, I helped her do her homework over the phone, then I took a good while to wash myself with wet wipes. There'd been no water for a long time. No one wanted to sleep and someone suggested looking for basements. We looked all over but didn't find any. But actually no basement would have saved us from Buratino and that kind of consoled us. At dawn they began storming the building with tanks. You cannot imagine how ecstatic we were. It meant they weren't going to use Buratino.'

We were going in deeper, closer and closer to Donbas. Passing wretched, tumbledown houses, broken-up roads and I'm thinking how depressing it all is. You say, 'it's depressing isn't it'. We drive on. We drive through a pine forest. I think, can't beat a pine forest. You say, 'can't beat a pine forest, can you'. We drive on.

We drive into Kirovograd. I've never been to Kirovograd, no one comes to towns like this unless they have to. We're in the military zone now, and you set up an interview for me with a famous battalion commander. For four hours he tells me funny and not-so-funny stories about Donetsk airport, for my research. He tells me things, shows me photos. He must have forgotten you shouldn't show civilians pictures of bodies ripped to pieces.

'Once we killed these three separatists and we thought we'd keep their bodies in one of the freezers left round the airport. We thought we might exchange them for some of their captives but no one ever came looking for them. So there they were, the three of them, stuffed in tight together. When we had new recruits they often tried to use that freezer as a table to eat off. And every time one of the more senior lads would come over and fling back the freezer door.

'We lost a captain on our last tour. We couldn't find his body. And then we all gathered for a briefing one day and suddenly in the complete silence a mobile rang. It wasn't one of ours. This childish ringtone ringing out in the derelict airport, no idea where it was coming from. We started to look and we found a body in the debris. It was the lost captain. His mobile was in his pocket and his mum was calling him. It was probably friendly fire that killed him, and his body had been hidden.'

We both stay in a hotel with the most totally inappropriate name: The Palatial. A twin room. You lie down on the bed on the right, lay your machine gun and handgun tenderly by the pillow, sigh a couple of times and fall asleep. Too quickly – you aren't pretending. You snore. I lie on hot coals all night. And not because I see before my eyes the photographs from the commander who forgot that you shouldn't show civilians pictures of bodies ripped to pieces by explosions. And not because you are snoring. I lie on hot coals for one reason only. I want you.

I think about how it could happen right now. You get up and come over to me. Or you stretch out your hand in the darkness. No, you say 'come here' in a commanding voice. And I step into your dark bed. But no. You won't call me. You lie there, surrounded by your weapons and snoring.

'I was injured, so I had to leave the airport with the lads who were leaving after their tour, going back to Peski. At the last moment someone threw a sack of kittens into the car. The mother had been killed in the fighting, the kittens were left and it was a shame to leave them, so we thought we'd take them with. Only we forgot to tell the driver. So we were driving along and we get into some trouble. They're shooting at us. The car is hit, and it keeps dying and the driver can't work out how to get it started again, and this bag of kittens opens and they're thrown about all over the car. The driver can't work out why the fuck the car's still going forward, like some mystic power at work. But when kittens start dropping off the ceiling on him then he loses the fucking plot. He thinks he's gone nuts, that we were bombed and this is hell. I can't tell him because I lose consciousness and when I come round I realise I'm in a field hospital. Where the rest are, the kittens, I haven't got a fucking clue. They ask me how old I am, medical history, and I answer automatically. Then I hear the nurse say to the surgeon "he'll do". They're about to inject the anaesthetic and operate. And I remember these stories about how they cut organs out of injured patients during operations and I feel for my grenade in my pocket, pull out the pin and hold it out. Listen you cunts, you operate without anaesthetic. If I get knocked out then you all go with me. They operate without anaesthetic, one of the doctors passed out, I never loosed my fucking grip on the grenade. The operation was a success.'

How strangely this love has come to me. In what strange association.

The road. Empty petrol stations. The first checkpoints. The first soldiers. The first armoured vehicles come towards us. The first night in the first military base. The officers eat kebabs, drink brandy, they have no motivation to fight. You have motivation and a guitar. I have a digital recorder and a racing heart.

When you take up your guitar I forget that one of my exes was a snob about guitar music and used to despise sing-alongs. We all watch you with adoring eyes and sing along tunelessly. Another officer films a clip and puts it on

Facebook. One hundred, two hundred, a thousand likes. Our women have gone crazy for soldiers this last year. Girl I know even got a tattoo: 'I heart the airborne.' And now I'm crazy, too.

The officer who filmed you hangs out on social media a lot. He put up a clip of himself coolly addressing the enemy from the airport under siege. He's got fifty thousand followers on Facebook. Women leave comments like 'my hero' and 'I want your babies'.

I spend the night in the officers' barracks, where no woman has ever set foot. I sleep on a camp bed in a sleeping bag. You snore on the bed beside me. I bet you can't even hear how you snore because you have concussion and you can't hear in your left ear. In fact all twelve officers are snoring, but we were drinking hard, so I nearly sleep.

There is no heating, no shower or toilet in this place. The nearest toilet is about three hundred metres through the mud. But there is a huge TV screen, given to them by some volunteers. Glamorous men and women slide across its screen from morning until night. Slick talk show hosts in fancy suits make jokes about politics. I wake up and I see the soldiers' backs. And yours. You're standing facing the screen, cradling a smoking coffee. I can get quietly dressed behind your back and even wash a bit with wet wipes.

Sometimes, when I fought with my ex-husband, I tried to imagine him going off to war, just to stop myself from totally hating him. I imagined his unhappy, intellectual back, a kitbag on his shoulder. I imagined him walking into the distance, like a scene from an old Soviet war film. I watched his receding back and I wept and I forgave him everything.

The men's backs in front of the TV screen are different. Straight and strong. But I still want to weep and forgive them everything.

Your straight back.

You look like there's an iron rod running through you. A ramrod, out of place in any normal kind of existence. And you look like a dried-up plant in the desert. When I look at you with all the love my sly writer's heart can muster, and you feel my gaze on you, it's as if you draw in water, your features seem to smooth themselves out. It doesn't last long, I see in that moment how lonely you are, how unused to human company.

There's nowhere to eat on the road to Mariupol. It's getting dark, the towns and villages are fewer and fewer. You want me to have some food. At last, at one of those wretched little roadside cafés we are served by three girls, probably still at school. The café is a hellhole, barely lit, but their young faces are shining in the darkness. They look like small, frightened birds.

'Once my mum and I were arguing in the corridor at home. She gets on my nerves because she doesn't take her shoes off at the front door, she walks all the way down to the living room and takes her shoes off there. She walks in all the dirt. We were having such a row, when suddenly there was an explosion. The first one in our town. It was terrifyingly loud. My mum and I forgot all about our fight. She threw herself at me, shouting, 'daughter, daughter!' We sat down in the doorway like they said you should in an air raid. My mum had hysterics, she was crying and she kept repeating 'daughter'. I will never forget that 'daughter', I'd never heard her speak that way before...

'When I was little there were more boys than girls in our yard. There were only two girls and the rest of the kids were boys. We used to play at weddings. A boy called Kostya made up the wedding game, he was the oldest of all of us. I was always the bride. And Kostya was always the best man. I wore a bit of net curtain on my head. Our parents brought out tables and wineglasses. My bridegroom Sasha sorted the food and drink. He used to love eating so that must be why he liked getting married so much. He wetted bread in water and sprinkled sugar on it. Once I couldn't find any net curtain so I got some scissors and chopped a bit off the new curtains in the hall. My mum didn't tell me off. She kept that bit of curtain and it's still there in the cupboard. But our best man Kostya was killed last summer. Hit by a bomb. I often remember our weddings.

'There was a family with a little girl down in the basement with us. She was about three perhaps. Explosions kept going off and her parents told her they were fireworks to stop her getting frightened. So then every time there was an explosion the little girl shouted "yay".'

The girls brought battered meat, potatoes and salad. You eat a double portion. You like meat and potato. The food is disgusting in the zone. I nearly vomited up the macaroni and meat at the military base by the sea where we ended up. So we eat on the beach: canned tuna you brought with you and bread. I don't know how many days we spent together, how many times we stood so close we could have kissed, or slept so close we could have held out our hands to each other. You must have come to a decision today though, when you took the canned tuna and wine down to the beach.

After Crimea was invaded last year we hardly had any sea left in our country. The Azov Sea is a pathetic little sea for the poor. There was a hotel here once. Now it's a military base for volunteers. An empty beach with pine trees along the shore. *Can't beat a pine forest…*

On the other side of the bay the sound of explosions, and beautiful grey clouds of smoke rise like fountains and spread along the horizon. Over there is the village of Shirokino and the front line. Over there right now, men are blowing each other to bits with rocket launchers. The March sun is so bright.

You kiss me for the first time. You decide when and how to do it. I decide nothing. My legs go weak. I can't stand. It feels like, this is fucking it, here it is, that very scene from the film about love, I have seen it and heard about it so many times, and felt it for others, but never for myself. Here you are, love. In your honour bombs are falling on the far shore. In your honour someone has just had their leg ripped off.

How crass it is to talk about love in war, to talk about the first kiss against a backdrop of firing. It's just like too big, too beautiful. I can just feel you're all cringing and at the same time you envy me… Shall I tell you about the sex?

I don't know what you'd do if you found out I was telling an audience in a theatre about us. Would you shoot me dead?

No, of course not. But I know that you'd be angry, and you'd break off all relations with me straight away. Still we hardly have a future together. I close my eyes and I see no future for us.

The way I live, my liberal views, all irritate you and your radical views frighten me. You are so jealous and you'll never ever admit it. An earnest young vegan loves me and is waiting for me at home in Kiev. And somewhere in Lviv there's another woman with big breasts who's waiting for you. She's younger than me, she has nail extensions and she knows how to cook pork.

I go on her Facebook page. She's a fucking idiot. She's always posting cake recipes and weight-loss suggestions. Like one day she'll post a cake recipe and literally the next post will be 'how to lose eight kilogrammes in a week'. And sometimes she posts these quotes by famous singers: 'so what if you're right when your lady is crying?' and 'your beloved knows no rivals in love' – and 'if a woman became a man and saw herself in his eyes she would fall in love with every inch of herself'. I mean what the fuck…

I think about you being wounded. I arrive at the hospital where *she* will also be. And another woman, perhaps. How will we all share you? Will we each take a bit of you? It'd be easier for us if you were already dead. She'll be the official mourner, weeping at the graveside. The others would stand to one side, we'd know each other by appearance, by the level of grief: she's in a state – slept with him twice. And the proud one in her black mourning dress – must be the first wife.

When my dad died five or six women came to his funeral and they all behaved like his widows. They took it in turns to speak, and made speeches… They talked about how he loved them and they loved him… And when he was being cremated, one of them came up to me and said, 'your dad owed me three hundred dollars.'

And my dad, he wasn't even a war hero, although at some point a long time ago he must have been an epic lover, but when he died he was a sixty-year-old invalid who'd had three strokes. Five women fought over him at his funeral.

I mean, if you're killed, think what it'll be like: a war hero, a leader of men, this guy at the peak of life... And when it's my turn to speak at the funeral – what will I say?

Ladies and gentlemen, fellow soldiers, brothers and sisters... When we first spent the night together he couldn't get it up. After a week of hanging on, sleeping in barracks, kissing on the beach, we made it to a flat with a sofa bed and a shower and clean linen. When you'd taken off your machine gun, your holster, stripped off your uniform and your underwear and slipped out of this hideous war... you couldn't get it up. It barely stirred. And I was terrified. And so once again you lay snoring and I lay awake all night. So this is war, I thought. This is the reality. And this is love. And I knew I could bear it, this love, even if it never happens, I'll just lie and smell you. You smell so good, I never knew a man could smell as good as you do. I wonder if you only smelt good for me, or for them, too. That's what I'll say. Or not say? No, I will say it, if you're okay with that. Because all the others will talk about the fantastic sex they had with you. You getting it up with them. And I need to be different in some way. You don't want me to? Well, I've said it now, I'm sorry... Don't shoot me. Relax. No one knows you here. I won't be there to bury you. It'll be someone else.

I'll kill you and mourn you in my script for a film about the siege of Donetsk airport. You were the one who told me why Cossacks have so many songs about death. They're rehearsing their own deaths in life, so they aren't scared when it comes. And they weren't scared... Maybe.

How about if you go to prison, if they put all the volunteers in prison? Will we wait for you? How will we all visit you? One by one? I would definitely be better out of that one. I'm just not up to fighting for my happiness.

But the unhappiest of all unhappy endings is you simply go back to Lviv and you're happy with your big breasts and the fake nails.

Jesus, I wish you a long and happy life!

Please. Can you give us a better ending, Mary?

You take off the little Ukrainian trident you wear round your neck and you fasten it round mine: the symbol of Ukrainian independence. You've worn it right through the war. The leather cord has soaked up the dirt and sweat from your body because when you were defending the airport you didn't wash for weeks. Every time I wash I will remember that. Then the cord breaks and I wear it on a chain. And then I lose it. But right now you are taking it off and hanging it around my neck like a medal. I feel how important this is. And I ask you how I can thank you. You lower me to my knees in front of the mirror in the corridor of the hotel and undo your flies. As much as you want, my love. A medal must be earned. I earn my medal and you watch in the mirror.

People do such funny things, you said afterwards. Yes, it probably did look funny, kneeling in front of a man in a uniform who was thinking of the task of a Ukrainian patriot. A Ukrainian patriot's task is to serve the people of Ukraine and keep the country united and independent. Not to get into politics but to make politicians serve their people and their country. To give up your life to keep the country united, if needs be.

Conviction is contagious, did you know – you can catch it through oral sex.

You drive me home. You know as well as I do that it will be a slow and painful parting: you from me, me from you. We, who were united for such a little time. And no fucking patriot is going to give his life to keep us together.

The woman at the petrol station offers us salted cucumbers on the drive home. She picked them and salted them last year during an air raid. She and her husband spent a week in the basement and between raids she would run out to the vegetable garden and pick the cucumbers so they didn't spoil. They were beautiful. Really beautiful. I was even sorry I don't drink vodka. I could drink it now.

2.

Three TEENAGE GIRLS *sit in front of a kiosk shop. They are chewing on sunflower seeds.*

During this scene the characters talk without any emotional pitch and they don't shout. They are all tired of loud noises. They speak calmly. The girl only shouts once: when the woman says the word 'Lord' – and even that isn't essential.

TEENAGE GIRL ONE. I got a lipstick off Adam.

TEENAGE GIRL TWO. Well Bison gave me shampoo and conditioner. Feel my hair.

They all feel her hair.

TEENAGE GIRL ONE. Silky-smooth. (*To* TEENAGE GIRL THREE.) What did yours get you?

TEENAGE GIRL THREE. Um. These. Seeds.

TEENAGE GIRL ONE. That doesn't count. That's just like seeds. What present did he get you?

TEENAGE GIRL THREE *sits silently chewing on seeds and looking into the darkness.*

TEENAGE GIRL TWO. Don't stress, he'll get round to it, won't he. You ask him for something. He's not mean.

TEENAGE GIRL ONE. If he hasn't given you a present by now, he's not going to.

TEENAGE GIRL THREE. He isn't mean.

TEENAGE GIRL ONE *and* TWO *exchange glances.*

He gave Uncle Kolya a sack of cabbage and a bucket of beetroot.

TEENAGE GIRL ONE. What's Uncle Kolya got to do with it? Is he *his* boyfriend then or something?

TEENAGE GIRL THREE. He's just not mean, that's all.

The others snort.

They chew on seeds and watch the soldiers going into the kiosk shop and coming out with their purchases.

TEENAGE GIRL ONE *becomes suddenly animated*.

TEENAGE GIRL ONE. There's their commander.

TEENAGE GIRL TWO. Yeah, I heard he blew up the checkpoint where Vovka's dad was posted.

TEENAGE GIRL ONE. He was after my mum.

TEENAGE GIRL TWO. Vovka's dad?

TEENAGE GIRL ONE. The commander. And Vovka's dad. They're all after her.

TEENAGE GIRL TWO. He's gorgeous.

TEENAGE GIRL THREE. The commander?

TEENAGE GIRL ONE. I suppose… Only she hates them. She beat me for going with Ukrainian soldiers.

TEENAGE GIRL TWO. I don't get hit. I take home brandy and cans of meat. (*To* TEENAGE GIRL THREE.) What about you?

TEENAGE GIRL THREE. Me neither.

TEENAGE GIRL TWO. Did you get in trouble?

TEENAGE GIRL THREE. Well a bit.

TEENAGE GIRL TWO. Did you?

TEENAGE GIRL THREE. Yeah.

TEENAGE GIRL TWO. The kids at school are boycotting me though. They called me a slut and Ukrainian-shagger. So I told them that Bison would come and do them and that shut them up. But no one goes for a smoke with me any more, or lets me copy their work.

TEENAGE GIRL ONE. How come they know?

TEENAGE GIRL TWO. Someone let the secret out. Some fucking bitch.

TEENAGE GIRL ONE. I reckon it was Krava. She's on everyone's case.

TEENAGE GIRL TWO. Bitch. We should get her after school tomorrow.

TEENAGE GIRL ONE. Go on then. I've been waiting for ages. Hey we could flush her head down the toilet.

TEENAGE GIRL TWO. Yeah.

TEENAGE GIRL ONE (*to* TEENAGE GIRL THREE). You with us?

TEENAGE GIRL THREE. I can't tomorrow.

TEENAGE GIRL TWO. Why not? We were on your side when Krol beat you up.

TEENAGE GIRL THREE. I'm not coming to school tomorrow.

TEENAGE GIRL TWO. Day after tomorrow then?

TEENAGE GIRL THREE. Maybe.

TEENAGE GIRL ONE. You've got a nerve.

TEENAGE GIRL TWO. Hey come on. Don't fight. I'm just pleased to be home from evacuation. I thought I'd go mad in Berdyansk. Like, it's cool, there's a beach there, but all I could think of was what was going on with the cat and Dad. And then I'm back and I'm in the street and I hear shooting and... I feel just great... Back home. Standing there with the biggest smile on my face. And then Bison comes along and says, 'What you thinking?! Are you shell shocked or something?! Get down in that basement!' That's how we met.

A whistle from the darkness. TEENAGE GIRL TWO *gets up, comes to life.*

I'll be seeing you then.

She kisses them and goes into the darkness. They sit for a while in silence.

TEENAGE GIRL ONE. I think it's right they aren't talking to her. He isn't her first, you know. She doesn't do it for love.

TEENAGE GIRL THREE. Are you doing it for love?

TEENAGE GIRL ONE. Yeah. I'm like that story about Juliet, everyone's against us and we're fighting on our own. Adam is my first guy. What about you?

TEENAGE GIRL THREE *is silent.*

Have you even kissed him? Go on, tell us.

TEENAGE GIRL THREE *is silent.*

You haven't even kissed him.

TEENAGE GIRL THREE *is silent.*

If you don't want to go all the way you can take it in your mouth or your arse. Only it hurts in your arse.

TEENAGE GIRL THREE *is silent.*

Lost your tongue.

TEENAGE GIRL THREE. No, I just don't want to talk about that stuff.

TEENAGE GIRL ONE. We're friends. If we can't talk about it then how will you find out about stuff?

TEENAGE GIRL THREE. I'll ask.

TEENAGE GIRL ONE. Want to know what my Adam says about your man?

TEENAGE GIRL THREE. No.

TEENAGE GIRL ONE. You should know.

TEENAGE GIRL THREE. When I need to know I'll ask.

TEENAGE GIRL ONE. Quit being so stressy. No-mates.

A whistle from the darkness, very different from the first.

TEENAGE GIRL THREE. Go on.

TEENAGE GIRL ONE. Adam. Right, I'm off. I'll tell you later anyway.

The girls kiss and TEENAGE GIRL ONE *goes into the darkness.*

TEENAGE GIRL THREE *remains sitting there on the bench. She stops chewing seeds. From time to time she hears whistles but they are not his. Other girls leave at each whistle.*

WOMAN ONE, *an elderly lady with a weary face and untidy grey hair, approaches. She sits carefully on the bench near* TEENAGE GIRL THREE. TEENAGE GIRL THREE *sees* WOMAN ONE, *and sulkily slides to the opposite end of the bench. She begins chewing seeds again and angrily spitting the husks on the ground. They remain like this for a while.*

WOMAN ONE. Give us a seed.

TEENAGE GIRL THREE *carries on silently chewing seeds, but at length she does stretch out the cone of seeds and she pours some onto* WOMAN ONE*'s palm. They both sit and chew the seeds.*

Hey, love. It's late. Come home.

TEENAGE GIRL THREE. What's there at home?

WOMAN ONE. We can watch some TV together. That *First Dates*.

TEENAGE GIRL THREE. I don't want to.

WOMAN ONE. You've missed it three times now...

TEENAGE GIRL THREE. I don't want to watch Russian telly.

WOMAN ONE. We'll watch something else.

TEENAGE GIRL THREE. There isn't anything else.

WOMAN ONE. We'll put a DVD on.

TEENAGE GIRL THREE. I don't want to. You go and watch something.

WOMAN ONE. I'm not going anywhere. I promised your mum I'd be there for you till you –

TEENAGE GIRL THREE. Till I what?

WOMAN ONE. Till you grow up, love.

TEENAGE GIRL THREE. Till I go mad. Go home.

WOMAN ONE *stays sitting there stubbornly.*

WOMAN ONE. I'm all you've got.

TEENAGE GIRL THREE. I know.

WOMAN ONE. No one else gives a shit about you.

TEENAGE GIRL THREE. No one gives a shit about you.

WOMAN ONE. True. Me, neither. Give us some more seeds.

TEENAGE GIRL THREE *gives her the seeds.* WOMAN ONE *takes them but doesn't begin chewing them.*

He doesn't give a shit about you either.

TEENAGE GIRL THREE. Uh-huh.

WOMAN ONE. This kiosk wasn't always here. Used to be just a bench here and I used to sit here with my friends and when the boys were coming home from work we'd wait for them here. Our boys coming home from the pit. It's all different now. He'll have his fun with you and he'll move on.

TEENAGE GIRL THREE. Go home, Nan, I'm not coming home now.

WOMAN ONE. You've got school tomorrow.

TEENAGE GIRL THREE. It's only PE first lesson. I can miss it.

WOMAN ONE. How long have you been waiting here? He isn't coming.

TEENAGE GIRL THREE. Course he won't come if you sit there frightening him off.

WOMAN ONE. He's scared of me?

TEENAGE GIRL THREE. He's not scared of anything.

WOMAN ONE. He's a fascist, that's why.

TEENAGE GIRL THREE. He's not a fascist.

WOMAN ONE. They'll slice us all up into salami when they retreat.

TEENAGE GIRL THREE. You're a bit old and stringy for that, Nan.

WOMAN ONE. I'm not worried for myself.

TEENAGE GIRL THREE. So why haven't they done it already?

WOMAN ONE. Because they get paid a lot.

TEENAGE GIRL THREE. They aren't going to retreat. Go home.

WOMAN ONE. Let me do your hair in a nice plait.

TEENAGE GIRL THREE. Don't touch me. If he comes, I'm going to pretend not to know you, I'll say I don't know you. And don't you dare say you know me.

WOMAN ONE. How can I do that? I know you. I've known you since you were born. When Lena had you I was sitting outside the room and praying. And when you were dying with the whooping cough I was praying for you then, and bringing you soup. And when you got lost at the shops I was –

TEENAGE GIRL THREE. You've got to stop praying for me! You prayed for Mum and she died. Everyone you pray for dies. Don't pray for me.

WOMAN ONE (*crossing herself*). Lord…

TEENAGE GIRL THREE. No!

Throws the cone of seeds in her face.

They sit in silence on the bench.

WOMAN ONE. I'll go to their HQ and tell them he seduced you and raped you. And then they'll put him away for life. They won't want him in the army then.

TEENAGE GIRL THREE. I'll put my head in the oven and turn on the gas. And I'll leave school…

WOMAN ONE. Yanochka –

TEENAGE GIRL THREE. Don't you dare cry here.

WOMAN ONE. I won't… Let's go home, I'll fry up some potatoes. We'll watch the TV.

TEENAGE GIRL THREE. No.

WOMAN ONE. Will you have a bit of soup at least?

She gets out a container of soup.

TEENAGE GIRL THREE. Put it away. It's like you're trying to show me up.

WOMAN ONE. No point in wandering around hungry. Go on, just have a bit. I promised your mother… If you eat it I'll go, do what you like, fuck who you want.

TEENAGE GIRL THREE *takes the soup and eats with an expression of disgust.*

TEENAGE GIRL THREE. I'm eating. Go now.

WOMAN ONE. What about the bowl?

TEENAGE GIRL THREE. I'll bring it back.

WOMAN ONE. Where will you leave it?

TEENAGE GIRL THREE. If you don't go home I'm not eating your shitty soup.

WOMAN ONE. Put it in this bag and leave it under that bush. And I'll come and collect it later.

TEENAGE GIRL THREE. Alright.

WOMAN ONE *leaves the bag and leaves, but it's obvious she hasn't gone far and is just standing under a tree.* TEENAGE GIRL THREE *eats the soup.*

The earth quakes with some sudden nearby explosions.

WOMAN ONE *returns quickly.*

WOMAN ONE. Did you hear that? They're firing at Debaltsevo.

TEENAGE GIRL THREE. So?

WOMAN ONE. He's not coming. They'll call him in.

TEENAGE GIRL THREE. Shit… It's all your fault. You came and that was it…

She angrily pours the soup over the ground.

WOMAN ONE. It's not my fault.

TEENAGE GIRL THREE. If he's killed I'll put my head in the oven.

WOMAN ONE. He'll survive.

TEENAGE GIRL THREE. How do you know?

WOMAN ONE. I just do.

TEENAGE GIRL THREE. If he's killed

WOMAN ONE. I'll pray for him.

TEENAGE GIRL THREE. You aren't praying right.

WOMAN ONE. Well I won't then. He won't get killed. They're only killing our lot.

TEENAGE GIRL THREE. He's mine.

A very big explosion close by.

WOMAN ONE. Will we go home or straight to the shelter?

TEENAGE GIRL THREE. Let's go home… No, I don't want to… Let's go to the shelter.

They walk slowly off to the shelter, TEENAGE GIRL THREE *looking all around, still hoping he'll come.*

3.

A Ukrainian checkpoint in Ukrainian territory, a little way back from the front line, next to a bombed out petrol station. A car travelling in the direction of the front line stops at the checkpoint.

An armed SOLDIER *wearing glasses checks the driver's documents:*

SOLDIER ONE. Passport.

> SOLDIER ONE *waits patiently. The* HEADTEACHER *offers his documents.* SOLDIER ONE *scans them. He lifts his eyes to look at the* HEADTEACHER.

Halyna?!

HEADTEACHER. I'm sorry?

SOLDIER ONE. Halyna Sergeevna, born 1975. Is that correct?

HEADTEACHER. Oh goodness, that's my wife.

SOLDIER ONE. Perhaps you've got her husband's passport as well?

> SOLDIER ONE *waits patiently while the* HEADTEACHER *looks.*

What's going on?

HEADTEACHER. I don't understand... I... picked up the passport this morning... It was on top of the fridge... I thought it was mine.

SOLDIER ONE. Step out of the car.

HEADTEACHER. Oh my goodness... Maybe you could ring my wife? She can confirm...

SOLDIER ONE. Have you got your licence?

HEADTEACHER. It was in the passport.

SOLDIER ONE. It's not here.

HEADTEACHER. Well no, that's my wife's passport. Oh goodness. Can I call her and you speak to her? She can confirm it all.

SOLDIER ONE. That's all we need. (*Speaks into his radio.*)
    We've got a driver without his documents here, commander.

The COMMANDER *emerges from the hut looking crumpled
and irritated. He is much shorter than* SOLDIER ONE.

Here.

He shows the COMMANDER *the passport. The*
COMMANDER *looks at it and then looks in the car.*

COMMANDER. So where's Halyna Sergeevna?

HEADTEACHER. She's at work. She's got a late shift at the
    hospital.

SOLDIER ONE. Got the passports confused. So he says.

COMMANDER. Step out of the car.

The HEADTEACHER *gets out. He staggers. The*
COMMANDER *sniffs.*

He's drunk as well…

HEADTEACHER. I'm local. I'm from Popasnaya, guys.
    What's going to happen?

COMMANDER. What do you think? Trying to cross a
    checkpoint in an conflict zone drunk and without documents.
    What do you fucking think's going to happen?

HEADTEACHER. We were having a drink with some of your
    boys. Our school won an army cadet competition and some
    of your boys came in to congratulate us…

COMMANDER. And what fucking school would that be?

HEADTEACHER. School Number Three. Over there, behind
    the block of flats.

COMMANDER. Keep your hands still.

SOLDIER ONE. Hands behind your back. Head down on
    the car.

SOLDIER ONE *pushes the* HEADTEACHER *into position
down on the car boot.*

COMMANDER. Open up the boot.

The HEADTEACHER *is lying on the boot.*

HEADTEACHER. Lie here or open the boot? For God's sake.

SOLDIER ONE. Open the boot.

The HEADTEACHER *gets up and opens the boot.*
SOLDIER ONE *examines the boot.*

HEADTEACHER. I'm the headteacher of School Number
Three, everyone knows me round here. Ask anybody.

COMMANDER. The thing is, headteacher, passports were
invented so there wasn't a need to go round 'asking
anybody' who you are. And in a war situation most people
don't even go for a shit without their passports, let alone
going for a motor round town. How did you leave the area?
Did you cross this checkpoint?

HEADTEACHER. What, on the way there?

COMMANDER. Did you hear me?

HEADTEACHER (*remembering*). I had my passport.

SOLDIER ONE. The one you left on the fridge.

HEADTEACHER. Oh, fucking hell, that means I must have
taken both, hers and mine... It's probably somewhere in the
car. Let me just... It could have fallen under a seat...

COMMANDER. That's known as contradictory evidence.

SOLDIER ONE, *who has been examining the contents of the
boot whistles loudly.*

SOLDIER ONE. Get a fucking load of this.

The COMMANDER *looks in the boot and whistles.*

(*Yells.*) Hands behind your back, face down on the car!

He pushes the HEADTEACHER *back down on the boot. The*
COMMANDER *gets a Kalashnikov out of the boot.*

HEADTEACHER. Listen guys, I know you're not going to
believe me... right, this is going to make you laugh... but
actually it's not real.

COMMANDER. What?

HEADTEACHER. It's a replica. It was presented to the kids.

COMMANDER. What kids?

HEADTEACHER. My kids, the ones at my school. The older ones.

SOLDIER ONE *examines the weapon*.

COMMANDER (*to* SOLDIER ONE). Is it a replica?

SOLDIER ONE. That's no replica. It's real.

HEADTEACHER. The soldiers from the local base presented it after the competition. To the kids.

COMMANDER. Right, so you're expecting me to believe that we're now arming children?

HEADTEACHER. It's a replica. For army training. Ring Major Kostenko.

COMMANDER. We don't have a Major Kostenko here.

HEADTEACHER. What do you mean? Aren't you the National Guard?

COMMANDER. We're the Krinitsky battalion.

HEADTEACHER. And you don't know Major Kostenko? Bald guy, missing a finger.

COMMANDER. Keep quiet for a moment.

SOLDIER ONE. What will we do, sir?

COMMANDER. I'll ring HQ. And you put him in the dugout. Spend some time down in the dugout with our rats and you'll sober up before you can say the word. I'll get the lot from security to sort this one out.

HEADTEACHER. But I've got to teach in the morning. Let me ring my wife at least!

COMMANDER (*on his radio*). Liberal, can you hear me… This is Anker. Yep… We've got a guy here drink-driving, no passport and a Kalashnikov in the boot. He says he's a headteacher. Making confused statements, yeah… Oh yeah.

HEADTEACHER (*shouts in desperation into the radio*). Major Kostenko, know him?! Who the fuck are you all fighting for?

COMMANDER (*shifting his attention*). What?

HEADTEACHER (*takes fright*). He's bald... he's got a finger missing.

COMMANDER. Who's got a finger missing?

HEADTEACHER (*cowering*). No one.

COMMANDER. Who are we fighting for?

HEADTEACHER. Alright boys. Lead me to the dugout. Do what you want. I'm guilty. Only let me call my wife.

COMMANDER. Personally I'm fighting so my daughter doesn't wake up one day to a war raging around her, like your children have. And so she doesn't have to hide in a fucking basement. Although I'm not actually fighting here, I'm just a wall between us and Mordor. But I will stand here and hold my ground until the last, I won't give in. And I'm also standing here to make sure that some drunken schoolteacher can't drive Kalashnikovs around the place. To make sure that teachers like that aren't let anywhere near children. Who knows what the fuck you're teaching them, which country you love. What flag you're travelling under...

The HEADTEACHER *nods but doesn't speak. The* COMMANDER *is in a real rage and calms down with difficulty.*

What am I fucking fighting for...

HEADTEACHER. I'm sober now, honest I am...

COMMANDER. Which school is it?

HEADTEACHER. It's a good school... Number Three. We're making camouflage netting for you. Weaving it.

SOLDIER ONE. Yeah, that's right. We went to get it.

COMMANDER. The security services will decide who's weaving what and why.

The HEADTEACHER *looks resignedly in the direction of the dugout. Suddenly he is animated by something he has seen.*

HEADTEACHER. Oh, Tanya, Tanya Marchenko.

COMMANDER (*tense*). What?

HEADTEACHER. A girl looked out of the dugout and it was one of my year eight students… (*Calls.*) Tanya! She'll confirm I am who I say I am… She's gone… (*Realising.*) What the fuck is she doing here?

COMMANDER. Lessons. What else would she be doing. We have a schoolkid in all our dugouts. You need to drink less.

HEADTEACHER (*bewildered*). But I saw Tanya… I'm sure.

SOLDIER ONE. Where should I take him?

COMMANDER. Send him home. Sleep it off. All his wild dreams. And tomorrow morning he can present himself with his passport. If you don't come we'll find you, even if you run away to Russia.

HEADTEACHER. Are you letting me go?

SOLDIER ONE. You sure?

COMMANDER. Get the fuck out of here. Leave the Kalashnikov. And the passport. Come back in the morning and we'll sort it.

HEADTEACHER. Just find Major Kostenko. He'll explain…

COMMANDER. Can you drive back?

HEADTEACHER. Slowly. And… glory to Ukraine!

COMMANDER (*through clenched teeth*). Just get out.

The HEADTEACHER *gets into the car and drives off slowly.*

SOLDIER ONE. Why did you let him go? He had a gun…

COMMANDER. It was a replica, wasn't it.

SOLDIER ONE. Really? Looked real.

They examine the gun.

COMMANDER. That was what the real ones used to be like. They use real old ones in schools. Didn't you do army training in school?

SOLDIER ONE. Nah… I went to the French specialist school.

COMMANDER. Fucking typical. No wonder the army is in the state it is… I used to be the fastest at stripping and reassembling them at school. Stopwatch?

   SOLDIER ONE *counts time and the* COMMANDER *assembles and strips the rifle.*

SOLDIER ONE. Fucking hell. Twelve seconds.

COMMANDER. Used to be eleven. Do it again.

   SOLDIER ONE *counts time and the* COMMANDER *assembles and strips the gun.*

SOLDIER ONE. Twelve. Hey he's coming back.

   A car approaches. The HEADTEACHER, *now sober, gets out.*

HEADTEACHER. I found my passport. It was under the seat. It had fallen down.

   The COMMANDER *examines the passport.*

COMMANDER. Well done you. Off you go then.

   But the HEADTEACHER *doesn't move.*

What? Oh yes, here.

   He gives the HEADTEACHER *the rifle. The* HEADTEACHER *holds it and immediately looks quite different. He doesn't move.*

HEADTEACHER. She's an orphan. She lives with her grandmother.

COMMANDER. Who?

HEADTEACHER. Tanya.

COMMANDER. What fucking Tanya would that be?

HEADTEACHER. Marchenko.

COMMANDER. You been smoking something as well?

HEADTEACHER. For God's sake Commander, it's wrong...
    I do understand that not all underage girls are the same... but
    all the same you should leave her alone. Her mother died...
    Her grandmother brought her up... You know what that
    means? It means they couldn't leave right through the
    bombing, they spent months living in a basement. She's not
    a good student, I'll grant you, and she smokes, but she isn't
    a whore.

COMMANDER. I think you're deliberately trying to fuck me
    off. Who do you take me for?

HEADTEACHER. Just let her come with me. I won't mention
    it to anyone. I'll just take her home.

COMMANDER. What a fucking nerve. I've got a wife and
    a daughter.

HEADTEACHER. No you're the ones with the fucking
    nerve... What are you doing to us? We want to believe in
    you... We need your support... My wife looks after soldiers
    every day in the hospital... One lot bomb us, the others fuck
    our children.

COMMANDER. I'll smash your fucking face.

    *They stand opposite each other, one holding a Kalashnikov
    replica, the other carrying real arms.*

I give you my word as an officer. She's not here.

    The HEADTEACHER *hesitates.*

Don't you believe an officer's word? Let's go then. You can
have a look round. Come on.

    The HEADTEACHER *hesitates.*

HEADTEACHER. There was someone in there.

COMMANDER. Two soldiers sleeping after their shift. And
    they keep a goose in there, too.

HEADTEACHER. It wasn't a goose.

COMMANDER. Don't you believe me?

The HEADTEACHER *so wants to believe him.*

HEADTEACHER. Officer's word?

COMMANDER. Officer's word.

HEADTEACHER. I'm sorry, Commander... You must be
right... My nerves I expect...

The HEADTEACHER *get in his car and leaves. The*
SOLDIER *and* COMMANDER *stand beside each other.*
They don't look at each other.

A camouflaged jeep drives up, coming from the front line.
SOLDIER TWO *at the wheel.* SOLDIER ONE *at the*
checkpoint salutes him. Then he bends towards SOLDIER
TWO *and says the first part of the password.*

SOLDIER ONE. Juventus.

SOLDIER TWO. Turin.

SOLDIER ONE (*referring to the* WOMAN *sitting beside him*).
With you?

SOLDIER TWO. She's our medic.

SOLDIER ONE. Can I see your passport?

He takes it and examines it.

Have a good trip.

SOLDIER TWO. Glory to Ukraine.

SOLDIERS. Glory to her heroes.

The jeep goes. SOLDIER ONE *is left. The* COMMANDER
disappears into the dugout.

4.

It is night. SOLDIER TWO *and* WOMAN TWO *are travelling in a camouflaged jeep.* SOLDIER TWO *is driving,* WOMAN TWO *sits by him. Both are in Ukrainian army uniform.*

WOMAN TWO. Can I put the radio on?

SOLDIER TWO (*looks at her in amazement*). Okay.

He searches the airwaves but can only find one channel playing tacky pop music.

That's all I can get.

WOMAN TWO. Leave it.

They drive on listening to the terrible music. The jeep shakes and rattles on the bad road.

SOLDIER TWO. There's a bad bit of road coming up.

WOMAN TWO. Oh, I remember it well. The road was like this before the war, believe it or not. When I was a student in Kharkov I used to come home this way at the weekend. Even back then it would knock the fillings out of your mouth. And they talk about the war – it's got nothing to do with the war.

SOLDIER TWO. I dunno, probably all the tanks and heavy stuff coming along has broken it up.

WOMAN TWO. Don't argue with me.

SOLDIER TWO. Okay.

They drive in silence, the conversation over.

WOMAN TWO. Listen, I'm sorry…

SOLDIER TWO. It's fine, I understand.

WOMAN TWO. It's just like this is all so absurd.

SOLDIER TWO. Grief, yeah.

WOMAN TWO. I said absurd. Wasn't me said grief.

SOLDIER TWO. Okay. Absurd.

WOMAN TWO. Keep your eyes on the road.

SOLDIER TWO *is silent.* WOMAN TWO *tries to swallow down her irritation.*

What did you do before the war?

SOLDIER TWO. Sport.

WOMAN TWO. So you mean you were a criminal?

SOLDIER TWO. A swimmer. Professional swimmer. How about you?

WOMAN TWO. Me? I had a travel agency. Sent people off to fry their arses on a beach.

SOLDIER TWO. I thought you did medicine.

WOMAN TWO. I just did a few courses at the beginning of the war. You've got a good body with all that swimming. Vitya had a nice body, but not because of swimming. He just did.

SOLDIER TWO. Uh-huh.

WOMAN TWO. He didn't even have to bother with weights or anything.

SOLDIER TWO *drives at low speed to avoid the potholes but it isn't possible and the jeep still shakes and rattles. He is silent and concentrates on the road.*

Vitya used to race along.

SOLDIER TWO. True. He liked a bit of speed.

WOMAN TWO. Do you know how we met, Vova? Your name is Vova isn't it?

SOLDIER TWO. Vladimir.

WOMAN TWO. Vladimir. Like Putin.

SOLDIER TWO. No. Like my dad.

WOMAN TWO. Is your dad still alive?

SOLDIER TWO. No.

WOMAN TWO. Well, Putin is.

SOLDIER TWO. Yeah, I'd swap them round...

WOMAN TWO. You can't.

SOLDIER TWO. I know.

WOMAN TWO. Can I drink?

SOLDIER TWO. We're not really supposed to but –

WOMAN TWO. I was joking. This is water.

WOMAN TWO *gets out a flask and takes a big gulp*.

What were we talking about?

SOLDIER TWO. About my dad.

WOMAN TWO. And before that?

SOLDIER TWO. You were talking about how your daughter came home.

WOMAN TWO. Yes...

SOLDIER TWO *turns the music down*.

We'd only gone into the block and she started crying and holding on to the walls, then the front door, and when we went into the flat she took off her boots and started pressing herself against the walls and the doors and the windowsills and all the rooms, and weeping and wailing like an old woman. She's only seven. I was following her and laughing and crying. I didn't know what to say to her. We'd only been away three months, went straight back after it was liberated. So I kept saying 'other people have been bombed out... they've got nothing to go home to...' and that set her off into hysterics... (*She is silent*.) Weren't we talking about how I met Vitya...

SOLDIER TWO. Oh... yeah...

WOMAN TWO. They gave us pills every day... Horrible pills. Lots of them. And he got fruit-flavoured vitamin tablets. I was crying because I kept missing home. And he came over and gave me his vitamin tablet. And I ate it. And then he gave it to me every day until we left...

SOLDIER TWO. I don't really get it...

WOMAN TWO. We were in hospital together when we were nine. An infection hospital in Kharkov. Horrible place.

SOLDIER TWO. Amazing. And it started then...?

WOMAN TWO. No. Not then... Thirty years later in the field hospital here...

SOLDIER TWO. And you recognised him?

WOMAN TWO. No. Not until later...

SOLDIER TWO. Jesus.

WOMAN TWO. He shouted at me when we first met. Because of that injured boy. But we couldn't have saved him. He was shouting from the start that I was to blame. Usually I give as good as I get, but that time I just burst into tears. That was my first KIA.

SOLDIER TWO. I was still in training then.

WOMAN TWO. What's it got to do with you... I was crying and he came over and gave me a sweet. Like he gave me that vitamin tablet when I was nine.

SOLDIER TWO *is silent*.

Say something.

SOLDIER TWO. You won't let me.

WOMAN TWO. Go on then.

SOLDIER TWO. He was a good commander. Upbeat, brave. Made everyone feel optimistic.

WOMAN TWO. Oh shut the fuck –

WOMAN TWO *doesn't want to listen to this, so she turns the radio up. She hums along, she drinks from the flask.* SOLDIER TWO *is already totally fed up by this journey, although it has only just begun.*

(*Shouting over the music*). He had a shit personality. He could give you this look and it was like a brick in your face. And then he'd get out the guitar and everyone loved him. And when he was drunk he was so tender, like a cat, said such beautiful things, the sort of things I'll remember till

I die. And on his arse he had a scar from an injection he'd
had as a kid, real deep scar. But I'd have recognised him
without that. I'd have recognised him by his fingers, his
nails, his knees. They didn't need to fucking DNA test the
body… Wasn't like I wasn't someone to him. Stop. I want
a pee. I've needed one for an hour now.

SOLDIER TWO *stops the jeep.* WOMAN TWO *gets out.*
SOLDIER TWO *turns off the engine. Silence. Something
rasps in the back of the jeep and* SOLDIER TWO *twitches
nervously.* WOMAN TWO *returns, she's frozen. She gets in.*

Christ, it's cold. My fucking pee froze.

SOLDIER TWO *tries to start the engine. It won't start. He
tries a few times.*

Is that a joke?

SOLDIER TWO. Hang on…

He tries again a few times.

WOMAN TWO. Why the fuck did you turn the engine off?

SOLDIER TWO. I wanted some quiet. You talking the whole
time, and when you're not talking then the music's
pounding. With my shell shock I can't get enough quiet.

WOMAN TWO. Usually you can't get enough noise when
you've got shell shock, you must be bad. Well that was daft.
What are we going to do?

SOLDIER TWO *tries again.*

Fuck this. Why don't I get out and push?

*She gets out without waiting for him to reply. He tries to turn
the engine on, she pushes. He gets out and pushes with one
hand and holds the steering wheel with the other. The jeep
starts to move, but the engine doesn't start.*

SOLDIER TWO. Let me try. And you steer.

WOMAN TWO *sits at the wheel and* SOLDIER TWO
pushes, but the jeep doesn't start. WOMAN TWO *stays in
the driving seat.* SOLDIER TWO *waits for her to move over
a little while, then gets in on her side.*

WOMAN TWO. Vova, yeah? Just don't say this is the first time this has happened, Vova…

SOLDIER TWO *doesn't reply.*

Fucking fantastic, minus twelve and I'm overnighting in a car with two guys. Dream come true.

SOLDIER TWO. We'll stop someone.

WOMAN TWO. Yeah right, it's like heavy traffic round here. Can't see for passing cars…

SOLDIER TWO *tries to ring.*

(*Mockingly.*) No reception, how surprising…

SOLDIER TWO. Yeah, it's my fault, I shouldn't have switched off the engine in the middle of nowhere.

WOMAN TWO *doesn't say anything. She tries to switch on the radio but it doesn't work.*

WOMAN TWO. Fuck.

SOLDIER TWO. It's my fault.

WOMAN TWO. It's not your fault, Vova. It's Vitya. He can't let me go. Remember that song – (*Sings.*) *'don't cry for me my darling, we still have a last night…'*

SOLDIER TWO. No, I don't remember that one.

WOMAN TWO. Oh yeah you're still just a boy. That was the song of our youth.

She drinks for a long time from the flask. SOLDIER TWO *switches on the hazard lights. They tick quietly in the silence. He looks out of the window in case a car comes past. They sit a little while in silence.*

It's cooling down fast in here, isn't it?

SOLDIER TWO. Here.

He takes off his camouflage jacket.

WOMAN TWO (*instantly*). Don't you dare. It'd be better if we fucked, Vladimir. Nothing personal, just to keep us warm.

SOLDIER TWO. What?!

WOMAN TWO. You used to come and get pills from the
    medical unit all the time and you'd watch me with hungry
    eyes. You fancy me, I know you do.

SOLDIER TWO. Yes, I liked you. But not any more. Your
    man's body in the jeep and you're trying it on with me.

WOMAN TWO. Ahaha... Would you prefer I tried it on
    with him.

SOLDIER TWO. Stop.

WOMAN TWO. He had a good body. But it doesn't turn me on
    now. And it's missing a head, isn't it. A body without a head
    in a body bag just doesn't turn me on.

She kneels on the chair and looks back into the jeep.

Vitya, where did you lose your head?

SOLDIER TWO. Don't drink any more.

WOMAN TWO. It's water. I don't drink on duty.

Takes a big gulp from the flask.

Come on, Vladimir, Vova, c'mon. It won't give me any
satisfaction anyway, I froze my clit off in the dugout on the
first tour... Me and Vitya we had strange sex, like a kind of
parody of sex. Sometimes he couldn't get it up and
sometimes it hurt me... Hard when you love someone and
you want them but you can't do it... But we did some
experimenting. Vitya, you remember all our games? C'mon
Vova, if only to make ourselves feel alive.

*She puts her hand briskly into his trousers. He instantly pulls
it out.*

SOLDIER TWO. Get out.

WOMAN TWO. Haven't you got any respect for your
    commander? His woman is cold – it's your job to warm her
    up. Or do you prefer boys? Is that why you're in the army, so
    you can hang around with men? Wash in a communal shower
    with some pumped-up smelly boys and go to sleep next to

them. You fancy the commander then, did you – go on, you
can tell me, gayboy.

SOLDIER TWO. Get out of the jeep fuck's sake.

WOMAN TWO. What? What did you say? You want a fucking
slap?!

SOLDIER TWO *jumps out of the car, opens the door and
drags her out of the car by the scruff of her neck.*

SOLDIER TWO. You piece of shit.

*He throws her out of the jeep, gets back in and locks the
doors.* WOMAN TWO *yells and bangs on the glass. Her
face is distorted by an expression of sheer hatred. A stone
hits the window.*

*She lies down on the bonnet, she jumps on it, she throws
stones at the window.* SOLDIER TWO *is beside himself with
rage and powerlessness.*

Fucking bitch, the fucking… cunt… the fucking…

WOMAN TWO *tires of all the craziness and slides down the
bonnet. There is silence.* SOLDIER TWO *carefully looks
down out through the window.* WOMAN TWO *leaps out,
her face still contorted, but now there is an element of
humour in her expression, rather than hatred. She slides
back down again. After a short while she reappears on the
other side. She begins passionately kissing the window by*
SOLDIER TWO, *she acts out scenes from the sinking of the*
Titanic. *He watches her with revulsion and horror. Then her
face suddenly empties of expression, becomes serious. She
turns and disappears into the night.* SOLDIER TWO *loses
her from view. He tries the engine again, but to no avail. He
checks his phone but there is still no reception.*

He begins to get worried about WOMAN TWO. *He opens
the door. He gets out.*

(*Calls.*) Lyudmila! Hey!

SOLDIER TWO *goes to look for her. There is the beep of an
arriving text message on* WOMAN TWO*'s phone, which is
in the glove pocket. The hazard lights tick.*

SOLDIER TWO *opens the door and helps lift* WOMAN TWO *into her seat. She sits down. She is weeping.*

Hey, ssshhh. You're cold? I'm so sorry, I'm so sorry.

WOMAN TWO (*like a child*). I've lost the pendant… Vitya's pendant… He gave me a pendant and I lost it in the snow by the jeep.

SOLDIER TWO. I'll find it, don't worry.

He gets out of the jeep and searches. She locks the doors.

WOMAN TWO. Vitya he's hurting me. He keeps hurting me, Vitya. Do something. I lost your pendant. I don't want him to see me crying.

She cries. SOLDIER TWO *knocks on the door and she gesticulates to him, making faces and gestures like a peevish, upset child.*

SOLDIER TWO *smokes by the jeep.* WOMAN TWO *gets out her phone and reads the text. She reads it a few times. She unlocks the doors.*

SOLDIER TWO *gets back in. He is shaking with the cold. She holds her phone. She isn't crying now.*

There must have been reception. And then it went. But I got a text. From Vitya.

She reads the text.

It says 'Find my head, Lyuda. Come back for my head.'

SOLDIER TWO. Give it here, I'll delete it.

WOMAN TWO. Jesus.

SOLDIER TWO. You know what it is… They've got his phone, they're playing games.

WOMAN TWO. Our texts to each other were on his phone. Pictures. Stupid stuff…

She reads texts from Vitya:

'Nvr ever shave ur pubes or ur armpits', 'I'm gonna lick u all over till my tong is num'

SOLDIER TWO (*gently*). Stop it.

WOMAN TWO. So they can read his texts but you can't, is that it? The last text from him read: 'I borrowd your cup wiv poppies on, sweetheart. XXX'. Animals. They cut his head off and now they're reading our texts. I'm coming back, you fuckers...

SOLDIER TWO. We'll come back together.

WOMAN TWO. I don't know how you can bury a person without a head... Hey why don't we cremate him...

SOLDIER TWO. Well that's for you to decide.

WOMAN TWO. No, I mean now. Burn his body, let it disperse in the air. It would be beautiful. Symbolic.

WOMAN TWO gets out of the jeep and opens the back door. She begins pulling the body bag out of the jeep. SOLDIER TWO grabs hold of the other end.

SOLDIER TWO. You've lost your mind.

WOMAN TWO. He's mine. I'll do what I want with him. And we can have a bonfire, keep warm. I'm so cold. Vitya would have kept me warm. But you don't want to.

SOLDIER TWO. C'mon now. I'll keep you warm. Come here, only calm down. We'll rip the body bag.

A tearing sound. WOMAN TWO *drops the body bag.*

WOMAN TWO. Oh God, Vitya, I'm so sorry.

She is in a muted hysterical state. SOLDIER TWO *gets out of the jeep and helps her get back in.*

SOLDIER TWO. Shhh. It's so cold he'll freeze... It doesn't matter. I've got spare bags in the boot. Come here, come here...

He hugs her and presses her close.

—

It is morning. SOLDIER TWO *is asleep, covered in his jacket.*
WOMAN TWO *is not in the jeep. She opens the door and sits
in her seat. She's composed, sober and wearing make-up.*

WOMAN TWO. Volodya, wake up.

He wakes up instantly, sits up.

The guys'll push us.

Someone is pushing the jeep. The engine starts. WOMAN
TWO *looks out of the window and waves to someone.*

Give me five minutes. (*To* SOLDIER TWO.) Stop the jeep.

He stops the jeep, but keeps the engine running. The
WOMAN *looks at him attentively.*

Did you dream of anything?

SOLDIER TWO. I dreamed I was so cold I couldn't sleep.

WOMAN TWO. I dreamt of those Ugg boots with sequins on.

SOLDIER TWO. What?

WOMAN TWO. Uggs, you know, those boots. I saw them on
this girl in Kiev when I was last there. All covered in sequins
and beads. I was drooling, I wanted those boots so much.
And I dreamed of them last night. I dreamed I was putting
them on and my feet were suddenly warm.

SOLDIER TWO. Shall we get going?

WOMAN TWO. No. I'll get a lift back with the guys to the
unit. You go on alone.

SOLDIER TWO. Why?

WOMAN TWO. Lera will get in at the next checkpoint.

SOLDIER TWO. Who's Lera?

WOMAN TWO. Vitya's wife. His widow.

SOLDIER TWO. But what about you?

WOMAN TWO. I'm no one. I was just accompanying him to
his relatives. But if you don't mind I'll get out here.

SOLDIER TWO. I didn't know.

WOMAN TWO. Men like him are always married.

SOLDIER TWO. You were like the ideal couple for me. Bastard.

WOMAN TWO. What?

SOLDIER TWO. He took four of the guys off with him... We all knew it was a crazy mission, but he took them with him.

WOMAN TWO. Don't speak ill of the dead.

SOLDIER TWO. Your Vitya was a bastard. Wife, lover... Fuck.

WOMAN TWO. Hey, you've still got to travel a bit further with him.

SOLDIER TWO. Fuck him. Did she know?

WOMAN TWO. I don't know. I don't care. He can hardly get divorced and marry me instead.

The beeping of a text. She shudders but doesn't look.

Fourth one today. Now they're threatening stuff.

SOLDIER TWO. Block that number.

WOMAN TWO. Block Vitya? I can't.

SOLDIER TWO. It isn't Vitya.

WOMAN TWO. It's like him continuing in some way...

SOLDIER TWO. I dunno... (*Pause.*) I'll get out, shall I? Don't you want to say goodbye?

WOMAN TWO. Only to you. I said goodbye to him last night.

SOLDIER TWO. I remember. I dreamed I kept covering you up.

WOMAN TWO. That wasn't a dream. You did keep covering me up. Thank you.

She kisses SOLDIER TWO *on the lips. She gets out.*

5.

*A door opens into a dark space, someone gropes for the switch
and a dim light goes on. A basement room with no windows.
Two people in the doorway.* HE *is wearing fatigues.* SHE *is just
a girl in a T-shirt and jeans.*

HE *never shouts at her, not even to frighten her, because* HE
knows it is more frightening when it is quiet.

HE. Here.

SHE. What do you think this was for?

HE. I think it was probably for storage.

SHE. What did they used to store here?

HE. What they store here now: equipment… for a sanatorium.
There's a bath there, and some shit here, not sure what it is…
Steam treatment maybe. I remember having those. Fucking
steam baths…

SHE. Is this like a spa?

HE (*laughing*). Fucking five-star resort.

SHE. So did they do medical stuff here too?

HE. Like what, treatments, do you mean?

SHE. Yeah, like curing musculoskeletal issues, or digestive
problems…

HE (*laughing*). Musculoskeletal, yeah that's right. (*Laughs.*)

SHE. I used to go to Mirgorod with my grandmother. We drank
the special water and had treat–

HE. Shut the fuck up and get undressed.

SHE (*immediately in tears*). You did it again… Just listen a
bit… My grandmother and me we went and had
treatments… we drank –

HE. Did you fucking hear what I said. Get your clothes off.

SHE. Please… Can I tell you how we went on holiday first…
Me and my grandmother… I had a back problem and every

year we went to this spa place and had mineral water from this drinking fountain and I had to wear a corset...

HE. You trying to make me sorry for you?

SHE. Well, you are human.

HE. I'm an animal.

SHE. You're a human. You had a steam bath, you said. You must have had a sore throat. I bet you hated it.

HE. You'll have a sore throat soon. My prick will see to that.

SHE. Let's not do that today. Please. I'll get used to it. Tomorrow I might be begging for it.

HE. I don't give a fuck when you're begging for it. I like it when... when you're howling.

HE *hits her in the face and* SHE *screams and cries even harder.*

See how that turns me on. Touch it, feel how hard I am. Feel it in your mouth.

HE *pushes her down onto her knees and forces her head in between his legs.* SHE *is crying so hard* SHE *is gasping for air.*

Give us some steam action then, you cunt.

SHE. Weren't you a kid once, too. Why are you like this...

HE. I wasn't a kid, I was a little shit, and now I've grown up I'm the full packet. The biggest shit.

SHE. You're not. You're a good man.

HE (*laughing*). Are you having a laugh? I'm a psycho. I like hurting things. I'm a sadist.

SHE. But isn't it hard to live like that?

HE. Are you sorry for me?

SHE. Yes.

HE. Suck me if you're so sorry for me.

SHE. I don't feel sorry for you like that. More like human compassion.

HE. Suck me then, Mother Teresa.

SHE. I'm sorry. I'm so sorry. I want you, I really do. Only I feel bad right now. I've got lots on my mind. Let's do it tomorrow, I'll do everything tomorrow… I really do like you.

His erection goes down and HE *starts getting really angry.*

HE. You a fucking lunatic? Or maybe you're some freaking Buddhist or something? Okay then. I'll fuck you in the arse until you shit yourself and then I'll put my prick right in your mouth and fuck you as you vomit and then I'll get the boys down here, a dozen filthy shell-shocked soldiers who've been living in fucking shit and haven't seen a woman in three months and they'll have you in every hole you've got. My mate Drone is so fucking well hung he'll shove his prick down as far as your kidneys. They'll pull you apart, bitch. Your mother won't recognise you by your knickers even.

SHE. My mother –

HE. Just don't say your mum died or I'll come in your face. Your fucking misery is turning me on. So what you say, you cunt? You keep talking, cunt.

SHE. I love you.

HE. Whatthefuck?

SHE. I love you.

HE *hits her hard.*

HE. You take me for some fucking dupe?

SHE. Do what you want. It just means you must have to do it…

HE *hits her.* SHE *groans but doesn't defend herself or put her hands over her face.* SHE *repeats as if in a dream:*

You're a good man. I love you. I love you.

HE *throws himself on her,* SHE *doesn't resist. For a while* HE *is occupied, but* HE *doesn't come.* HE *gets up.*

I love –

HE. Shut up fuck it I can't keep it up.

SHE. I'm sorry.

HE. You think you've won, you crafty bitch? Fucking journalist.
You reckon you're going to be writing about this on your
fucking Facebook page how you were taken prisoner and you
fucked The Phoenix. You'll come out of here in a box. And on
your page all that anyone's writing is 'How horrible.' 'What a
terrible death.' 'Her whole life ahead of her…' and '…she's to
blame what the fuck did she go there for anyway'.

SHE. I'm sorry.

HE. My men aren't going to give a shit if you resist or not. I'm
the only fucking pervert round here. They'll fuck you to
death. You wait here and get ready. Or bash your brains out
on that bath. They'll be coming in here one by one.

HE *spits on her and leaves.* SHE *lies there without moving.*
Then at last SHE *moves and sits up.* SHE *moans. The door*
opens. It's him again. SHE *freezes.* HE *comes over to her*
and urinates on her. Then HE *leaves.*

SHE *lies there a while, then gets up, sits and howls in horror.*
The door creaks. SHE *looks at the door.*

—

HE *comes back in with a tin of meat and a knife.* SHE *is wearing*
the same clothes only they are dirty, her hair is messy and SHE *is*
sitting in the corner of the room on a piece of material.

SHE *looks at him.* HE *opens the can with the knife.*

HE. I'll put it on the ground. You can eat from it like a dog.

SHE. Can I eat like a cat? Only I had a cat when I was a kid…

HE. Shut the fuck up about your fucking childhood. I had a
fucking hamster, where does that leave me…

SHE. What was its name?

HE. Fluffy. Bit me on my finger and I ripped his teeth out. Then
his paws. Drowned in its own gore.

SHE. That's not true.

HE. You want to be like that hamster?

SHE. I... I also... I ran over a chicken recently.

HE. What a fucking mess.

SHE. I was driving and it ran across the road... And I...

   SHE *sobs*. HE *cries a while*.

HE. You're a freak.

SHE. I stopped. I got out of the car and went into the yard.

HE. What yard?

SHE. The one the chicken ran out of.

HE. What the fuck.

SHE. To say I'd killed it.

HE. Did they tell you you were a freak?

SHE. They told me to pay them two hundred griven.

HE. Right. They got you were a freak straight away. A kilogram of chicken is only fifty griven. Just the meat. So a whole chicken isn't worth more than thirty.

SHE. I killed it though.

HE. Makes you a murderer, baby.

SHE. Yes.

HE. What if like I went into the front yards of all the Ukrainians I've killed... I'd be like 'I killed your son. How much did he weigh and how much per kilo?' What price would you put on a kilo of your lot?

SHE. Thousand.

HE. Are you having a laugh? If good quality chicken costs fifty a kilo then a fucking disgrace of a Ukrainian is twenty-five. The chicken never did anyone any harm.

SHE. It's only to you he's a fucking Ukrainian. For his parents and his country he's loved and cherished.

HE. Maybe you're right, sweetheart. Okay, let's say a thousand.
So how much does the average Ukrainian weigh?

SHE. Seventy kilos.

HE. Seventy times a thousand. Seventy thousand griven. Shit.
I've got fucking debts. No one could cost that much. Else
I owe about a million.

SHE. You couldn't owe that much.

HE. Okay, okay. So not a million, but a lot. Why aren't you
eating?

HE *gives her the tin of meat with a knife stuck into the
contents.* SHE *eats greedily from the knife.* SHE *holds the
knife and eats from it.* HE *walks around the room and
counts.*

Course it's a million. Have you forgotten your maths? Even
if you reckon on me having done for about thirty men or
so... that would be two million ten thousand. Well okay, not
everyone costs the same, some would be cheaper, some more
expensive. People come in different sizes.

HE *stands with his back to her.* SHE *looks at him.* SHE *has
stopped eating.*

Two fucking million, get that. Like some gold heist or
something. I'm on Interpol's books. But I'm a hero back at
home. My mum will get a letter... Like, we have an arrest
warrant out for your son because he's killed thirty Ukrainian
soldiers, with a total weight of two thousand, one hundred
kilos...

SHE. So what will your mum say to that?

HE. Mum's in shock. She's happy, she's proud. She gets a medal
and a certificate as a reward for bringing me up so good. They
want her to have more kids. And she says, you having a
fucking joke I'm fifty-five and I'm well past babies...

SHE. People have babies at fifty-five now.

HE. There you are. They tell her they have the best medical care
and all that shit.

SHE. You'd need the same dad. Otherwise the sons would be different. You couldn't rely on it...

HE. Hahaha... The same dad. He's pissed the whole time. He couldn't get it up if he wanted to. So what now?

SHE. Well it looks like you are unique, then. A one-off. Nobody like you in the whole world.

HE. A one-off?

SHE. Looks like.

HE turns suddenly towards her, reaches out. SHE licks the knife and gives it back to him.

HE. You're funny, you are. Only I bet you're shit in bed. You don't get me going. Are you a virgin?

SHE. I'm twenty-six.

HE. Who the fuck would fall for you? I mean you're not bad-looking or nothing, got a nice figure. But you don't turn me on. Don't know why the fuck you're coming on to me. Fucking crafty bitch.

SHE. You're my kind of man.

HE. I'm your type?

SHE. Yeah. When I saw you I thought someone like you couldn't be fighting on their side.

HE. I get it, you think we're all psychos and oddballs? I went to college.

SHE. I can see.

HE. Half my men have been to college.

SHE. You always idealise the soldiers on your own side.

HE. Fucking obvious. Your lot don't take girls prisoner, or gang rape them or put them up against the wall and shoot them.

SHE. Of course not. They're on our side.

They laugh together.

HE. I wasn't going to join up. I was going to build a house. I kind of had my own business. As a builder. The most peace-loving fucking business there is. I built palaces for people. But you fuckers forced my hand: what side to take, what songs to sing...

SHE. You remind me of this boy in my class at school. Sasha. I liked him.

HE. I wasn't your school friend. I'm your enemy. You came here to write your fucking stories about us. You dream of wiping us off the map.

SHE. If only we'd met two years ago. Before all this.

HE. I wouldn't have given you a second glance.

SHE. I was different then. You'd have liked me.

HE. Well I was different, too. You wouldn't have liked me. I used to hold hands with the girls, sit on park benches. And you like to be humiliated.

SHE. I was different too.

HE. Exciting? Sexual? Different smell? Are you Jewish by any chance? No you're not Jewish. I can sniff out a Jew. Everything bad comes from the Jews.

SHE. I don't agree.

HE. Fucking liberal... Gay parades, all that shit, eh?

SHE. Gays and Jews never did me any harm.

HE. Well the reason you're here, that's all their doing. You think it's sex...? They can fuck who they like as far as I'm concerned. It's not about sex, it's about power, about universal rule. Because under the beautiful pretence of their 'European values' they're making wars and making nations like ours – like brothers – fight, they're trying to destroy the power of the people who uphold real values, like family and religion and equality...

SHE. Destroying the power of goodness?

HE. What?

SHE. Gays and Jews are destroying the power of goodness?

HE. Yeah, brothers fighting brothers, spilling each other's blood, that's their doing. All your fucking Maidan.

SHE. Hang on, what about Americans?

HE. Yeah, them, too.

SHE. And fascist plotters? And nationalists?

HE. Don't take me for an idiot.

SHE. I don't.

HE. You want me to be an idiot. Like I'm just generalising and putting everything in one pile. It's just a really big pile. Because there's a lot of evil in the world and it's in power. They're like helping each other out, getting their own lot in power. They're defending themselves with their laws and their police and their human rights... Democracy is a cunning god, those fucking snowflakes and queers thought it up, so we all have to pray to it and they're hiding behind it like it's a wall and feeling fucking smug.

SHE. Where's the truth?

HE. There is a truth, only it's in the fucking arse-end of the world where the poor people, the real people live. I can prove with facts every single point I'm making.

SHE. No need.

HE. Afraid of losing the faith? Giving up your 'European values'?

SHE. I only believe in one thing...

HE. Yeah?

SHE. In goodness.

HE. Well, that's a fucking waste of time. There's none here, that's for sure. You know so much, you've seen so much, you won't get out of here alive.

SHE. You just proved to me that you're on the side of goodness. On the side of the poor people, family, religion.

HE. Yeah. But that doesn't mean I'm good.

HE *holds a knife to her throat.*

Now you're going to tell me that gays are evil. That Jews, Americans and Ukrainians are evil. And Maidan is evil. And Ukraine doesn't exist.

SHE. Yes, it's evil, it is. No it doesn't exist. Ow.

HE. Does it hurt? Now I'm going to gouge your eyes out.

SHE *collapses in a faint.* HE *slaps her cheeks.*

Are you stupid? That was a joke...

—

HE *comes in with a pail of water and a jug.*

HE. I'm going to wash you. You're covered in piss.

SHE. Okay.

HE. Get undressed.

SHE *obediently gets undressed.* HE *watches.*

SHE. I can do it myself.

HE. Leave it.

HE *pours water from the jug on her.* SHE *winces.*

Too hot?

SHE. Yes. Ow.

HE. Sorry. It'll cool down.

HE *pours hot water on her head.*

You'll be nice and clean. You've got a nice arse. Just the right size. But I don't like nipples like yours. Pale ones. I like them when they're big and dark-brown, so when you touch them they feel like that material they put in coffins.

SHE. Velvet?

HE. That's it. Like velvet. Or butterfly wings. How do you get rid of your pubes?

SHE. Epilation.

HE. Fuck. Is that like a laser?

SHE. No, they put wax on and then they peel it off.

HE. Hurts?

SHE. Yeah.

HE. You like it when it hurts.

> HE *pinches her nipple.*

SHE. Ow.

HE. Ow. That's giving me a hard on.

> SHE *looks at him frightened.*

> I'm joking. I wanted to check you loved me. You love me, right?

SHE. Right.

HE. I had this dream that you and me were at the butcher's together and looking at meat. I haven't dreamt about anything apart from war for a long time. And you say, let's get veal. But I say, pork. I love pork. So we get pork, of course. And then we get some salad and tomatoes. Tomatoes like, this big! My nan had –

> HE *falters.*

SHE. What was your nan's name?

HE. Lyuda.

SHE. Mine was called Valya.

HE. She was really kind.

SHE. All grandmothers –

HE. No they aren't!

> HE *is silent.* SHE *trembles with the cold.*

> HE *seems to be crying.*

SHE. I'm getting cold, Oleg.

HE. Are you losing your fucking mind? I'm not Oleg.

SHE. It's just really frightening when you cry. I just said it because I was frightened.

HE. Yeah, but why the fuck Oleg? It's a fucking pervert's name... My name is Stas.

SHE. Mine is Yulia.

HE. I know. I've got your papers. Yulia. Yu-li-a. Get some clothes on, Yulia. Here.

HE *gives her a set of men's fatigues.*

Smallest there was.

SHE *puts them on.*

You become an animal.

SHE. Me?

HE. No. Me. See stuff you never wanted to see. Even death. Death, you know, death can be easy. We're kind of used to death being like the fucking be-all, like the height of terror... You never forget the first time you see a mate killed in action. But you can take a ring off the finger of the tenth. I didn't take the ring. I just mean you're not shocked any more. Just happy it wasn't you. And then you can't even feel happy because you can't feel anything any more. The depths are more frightening than death. You look down and you think you've seen the lowest point. But you're fucking mistaken, there's another lower point under that one. And then another... And under that there's a dead comrade with his eyes gouged out... Who did that to him? A person, another human. And then you go and eat. You eat meat from a can and you think, the next prisoner I take, I'll gouge his eyes out. Alive. You get me?

SHE. Yes.

HE. You don't get fuck. And there's no way back.

SHE. I know a way back.

HE. What the fuck do you know? You couldn't even get out of here and the door's open.

SHE. I know.

HE. Well fuck off then. There's no one else around apart from us. Go.

SHE. I'm not going without you.

HE. Where are you going with me, crazy lady?

SHE. I don't know. Anywhere.

HE. I'm sick in the head. Get out, go on, while I'm letting you.

SHE. Any trauma can be turned into experience.

HE. And what do I do with this fucking experience?

SHE. I don't know. I've just read it, that all trauma can be turned into experience and can help you live life further…

HE. You're making it up. This experience never helped anyone. It just brings the end of the world nearer.

SHE. You had a dream of a time before war today. So something is left. It's a sign. Hope.

HE. Yeah, that was a funny dream. Only I didn't tell you the rest… I start getting the meat ready for the barbecue and it's got maggots crawling all over it.

SHE. You just made that up.

HE *laughs*. HE *is sitting on the side of the bath*.

HE. Come and sit with me, Yulia.

SHE *sits by him*. HE *looks at her*.

Like a park bench.

SHE. More like a wall. A bench is a bit wider.

HE. You're right. Like a wall.

HE *puts his arm around her shoulders. They sit like that a while*.

Hope? Was that it?

SHE. Yes.

HE. Idiot. Are we going to kiss?

SHE. Okay.

> HE *kisses her. Long kisses with pauses between them.* HE *strokes her shoulder. They sit like this, kissing like lovers on a park bench, or a wall in a small town, on their first date, straight from the cinema.*

HE. I'm not even going to touch your breasts. Do you like that?

SHE. Yes.

HE. Can you hear?

SHE. What?

HE. Cicadas.

SHE. Yes.

HE. Fucking amazing.

SHE. Wait there a moment.

HE. Okay.

> SHE *gets up and goes behind him.*

SHE. Don't look, okay?

HE. I won't.

> SHE *picks up a brick*

SHE. I'm so scared of you.

HE. What?

> SHE *hits him on the back of the head hard, a few times.* HE *falls into the bath.* SHE *spits on him, without any force, a girl spitting, a comic note in the tragic scene. Then* SHE *urinates on him with her two legs up on the sides of the bath. Then* SHE *sits for a while and cries. Then* SHE *takes his gun and leaves the basement.*

6.

Before the war.

*A GIRL who has been crying knocks on a wooden gate on
a road. A woman (VASYA'S WIFE) comes out to the gate.*

GIRL. Hallo.

VASYA'S WIFE. What do you want? We don't open the gate to
   people from the road. Were you raped? I can call the police.

GIRL. No need. I… I ran over your chicken.

VASYA'S WIFE. So?

GIRL. It's dying.

VASYA'S WIFE. And what do you want from us?

   The GIRL sobs.

   Vasya, come here! This girl says she ran over our chicken
   and she's crying!

   VASYA *comes to the gate. He looks at the GIRL suspiciously.*

VASYA. What do you want?

GIRL. I was driving and it threw itself under my car.

VASYA. What you saying? Sounds a proper kamikaze chicken.
   More like you were driving too fast and you weren't looking
   where you were driving.

GIRL. Well it's dark. And it ran out suddenly.

VASYA. So what do you want from us now? You run our
   chicken over and then you come here. You want me to say
   thank you?

GIRL. I know I can't bring back the chicken. But I'm happy to
   pay for it.

VASYA. This is a fucking circus.

VASYA'S WIFE. So which chicken is it?

   VASYA'S WIFE *opens the gate and goes out onto the road.
   She returns carrying the dead chicken.*

   It's our little layer.

GIRL. I'm so sorry... Oh God, what a nightmare... I've got a parrot at home myself. Oh! Look, it's still moving. Is it alive? Let's take it to the vet's! Only put it in a box so it doesn't get blood on the car seat.

VASYA *exchanges glances with his* WIFE. VASYA *leaves and returns, but with an axe rather than a box. He puts the nearly-dead chicken on the path and chops its head off. The* GIRL *screams.*

VASYA. Put it out of its misery.

GIRL. But what if... it could have been saved?

VASYA. Oh right. Put a bandage on it and push it round in a wheelchair, take it to a sanatorium...

The GIRL *is very stressed, she has never seen a chicken being killed before. She weeps bitter tears.*

GIRL. Yes... I see... How much do you want?

VASYA'S WIFE. I don't know, Vasya. But she was a good layer.

VASYA. A hundred griven, and get going.

VASYA'S WIFE. Vasya!

VASYA. Well I don't know. How much then. I've never sold a chicken like this before.

VASYA'S WIFE (*firmly*). Two hundred.

GIRL. Okay. Hang on.

VASYA *and his* WIFE *watch her open a pretty bag and get out a pretty purse and open it. It is empty.*

Oh goodness, I haven't got any cash... I bought some honey... Only a card.

VASYA'S WIFE. Vasya, do we accept credit cards? No I don't think we do.

GIRL. I... So embarrassing... Is there a cash machine anywhere nearby?

VASYA. She's having a laugh.

GIRL. Oh God... I'll bring the money tomorrow.

VASYA. I see.

VASYA'S WIFE. 'She'll bring it tomorrow...' This is some kind of scam. Go on with you, girl. Let it keep you awake at night.

GIRL. I'll go now, get some money out in town and I'll come back. Two hundred.

—

The GIRL *knocks on the wooden gate.* VASYA'S WIFE *comes out.*

VASYA'S WIFE. Well look at that, she's back.

GIRL. Of course I am, I made a promise.

VASYA'S WIFE. These days every one makes promises but no one keeps them. Starting with the president and right down to all the rest.

VASYA. Who's that?

VASYA'S WIFE. It's her.

GIRL. It's me. Here.

She gets out two hundred griven. They look at her.

VASYA'S WIFE. I've already plucked it. I thought we'd have enough for borshch, but you'd flattened her and I couldn't do any more than feed her to the dogs.

GIRL. How horrible...

VASYA'S WIFE. It's not easy when you're poor.

VASYA'S WIFE *does not accept the money.*

She laid upward of thirty eggs a month. Like our golden goose, she was. A dozen eggs is about thirty griven, so we are going to lose around a hundred a month. Take that for the year and we're losing one thousand two hundred griven. She could have kept laying for about two years, that's two thousand four hundred.

GIRL. Oh... I haven't got that much...

VASYA'S WIFE. I mean you'd think just a simple chicken. But she was keeping a whole family alive.

GIRL. I've got a thousand here. Of course I never imagined that a chicken could cost –

VASYA'S WIFE. And then I used to talk to her. Not with the other chickens, but I did with her. She was more than just a chicken.

VASYA'S WIFE *doesn't accept the thousand griven which the* GIRL *offers her.*

What if I was to run over your parrot?

GIRL. I haven't got that much on my card. I took out all the money I had.

VASYA'S WIFE. Vasya!

VASYA *comes out.*

She's only got a thousand.

VASYA (*tuts*). We'll have to ring the police and prosecute, or we'll lock you in our basement until your family arrive with some proper money.

GIRL. Are you serious?

VASYA. It was you who killed the chicken.

GIRL. I can give you my bracelet if you want?

VASYA'S WIFE *takes the* GIRL*'s arm and examines the bracelet.*

VASYA'S WIFE. What is it?

GIRL. Silver.

VASYA'S WIFE. That's not worth much.

GIRL. Actually it is worth a bit.

VASYA. How much?

GIRL. I don't know. It was a present.

VASYA. What's that round your neck?

GIRL. That isn't worth anything, but it has sentimental value.

VASYA'S WIFE. It's gold.

GIRL. It isn't.

VASYA'S WIFE. I know gold when I see it. Take it off, let me look.

GIRL. But… it was given to me by someone who loves me.

VASYA (*threateningly*). We loved our chicken.

The GIRL *takes off the chain from around her neck. She gives them the bracelet, chain and a thousand griven.* VASYA'S WIFE *takes it all and places it in her apron pocket. They look the* GIRL *up and down. Still they don't dismiss her.*

GIRL. I'll come back tomorrow and buy back the jewellery. Okay?

They are silent. They look at her.

Can I go please?

VASYA. Where?

GIRL. Home.

They don't answer. VASYA *takes her handbag. He and his* WIFE *examine the contents. The* GIRL *is very frightened.*

VASYA. Look at this.

VASYA'S WIFE *opens a make-up bag and takes out a pretty powder compact. She sniffs the perfume.*

GIRL. You can keep that if you like.

VASYA'S WIFE. I do like. Thank you.

She puts it into the apron pocket. VASYA *takes out the car keys.*

VASYA. What have you got in your car?

GIRL. In the car? Only honey. I bought honey. Would you like it?

VASYA'S WIFE. No thank you. We have honey.

VASYA. Nice car. Pricey.

The GIRL *can't quite believe they want the car. Then she can.*

A neighbour's child starts crying and a woman calls her husband: 'Darling, Marina's crying. Go and see, I've got my hands in dough.'

VASYA *and his* WIFE *turn towards their neighbour's house.* VASYA'S WIFE *shakes herself, as if shaking off a bad dream. She thrusts the bag and the car keys at the* GIRL.

VASYA'S WIFE (*angrily*). Get out of here… like a bleeding headless chicken. Go on with you! Don't tempt us.

She pushes her away with force and shuts the gate behind her.

A Nick Hern Book

Bad Roads was first published in Great Britain in 2017 as a paperback original by Nick Hern Books Limited, The Glasshouse, 49a Goldhawk Road, London W12 8QP, in association with the Royal Court Theatre, London

Bad Roads copyright © 2017 Natal'ya Vorozhbit
Translation from the Russian copyright © 2017 Sasha Dugdale

Natal'ya Vorozhbit and Sasha Dugdale have asserted their right to be identified respectively as the author and translator of this work

Cover design by Root

Designed and typeset by Nick Hern Books, London
Printed in the UK by CPI Books (UK) Ltd

A CIP catalogue record for this book is available from the British Library

ISBN   978 1 84842 714 3

CAUTION   All rights whatsoever in this play are strictly reserved. Requests to reproduce the text in whole or in part should be addressed to the publisher.

Amateur Performing Rights   Applications for performance, including readings and excerpts, by amateurs in the English language throughout the world should be addressed to the Performing Rights Manager, Nick Hern Books, The Glasshouse, 49a Goldhawk Road, London W12 8QP, *tel* +44 (0)20 8749 4953, *email* rights@nickhernbooks.co.uk, except as follows:

Australia: Dominie Drama, 8 Cross Street, Brookvale 2100, *tel* (2) 9938 8686, *fax* (2) 9938 8695, *email* drama@dominie.com.au

New Zealand: Play Bureau, PO Box 9013, St Clair, Dunedin 9047, *tel* (3) 455 9959, *email* info@playbureau.com

South Africa: DALRO (pty) Ltd, PO Box 31627, 2017 Braamfontein, *tel* (11) 712 8000, *fax* (11) 403 9094, *email* theatricals@dalro.co.za

USA and Canada: Casarotto Ramsay and Associates Ltd, see details below

Professional Performing Rights   Applications for performance by professionals in any medium and in any language throughout the world (including by stock companies in the USA and Canada) should be addressed to Casarotto Ramsay and Associates Ltd, Waverley House, 7–12 Noel Street, London W1F 8GQ, *fax* +44 (0)20 7287 9128, *email* agents@casarotto.co.uk

No performance of any kind may be given unless a licence has been obtained. Applications should be made before rehearsals begin. Publication of this play does not necessarily indicate its availability for amateur performance.

MIX
Paper from
responsible sources
FSC   FSC® C013604
www.fsc.org

www.nickhernbooks.co.uk

facebook.com/nickhernbooks

twitter.com/nickhernbooks